THE
INTIMATE
MACHINE
Close Encounters
with Computers
and Robots

THE
INTIMATE
MACHINE
Close Encounters
with Computers
and Robots

by

Neil Frude

NAL BOOKS
NEW AMERICAN LIBRARY
TIMES MIRROR

For information address The New American Library, Inc.

NAL BOOKS TRADEMARK REG. U.S. PAT. OFF. AND FOREIGN COUNTRIES
REGISTERED TRADEMARK—MARCA REGISTRADA
HECHO EN HARRISONBURG, VA., U.S.A.

SIGNET, SIGNET CLASSIC, MENTOR, PLUME, MERIDIAN AND
NAL BOOKS are published by The New American Library, Inc.,
1633 Broadway, New York, New York 10019

Library of Congress Cataloging in Publication Data

Frude, Neil.
  The intimate machine.

  Includes index.
  1. Microcomputers. 2. Artificial intelligence.
3. Electronic data processing. I. Title.
QA76.5.F76 1983   001.64   83-8344
ISBN 0-453-00450-4

Designed by Leonard Telesca

First Printing, September, 1983

1 2 3 4 5 6 7 8 9

PRINTED IN THE UNITED STATES OF AMERICA

Contents

Introduction:
The Illusion of Life

The scene is a New York vaudeville parlor in the early years of this century, and a crowd has gathered to witness a new miracle. The performer appears to draw on a white board. The shape gradually becomes recognizable as that of a dinosaur. The artist introduces her as Gertie, and then, amazingly, she bows to the audience. Apparently in response to the performer's commands, the beast lifts a paw, takes a drink, and dances.

This "miracle" was achieved by the back projection of a cartoon film, and the performer was the pioneer animator Winsor McCay. His apparently spontaneous patter was carefully rehearsed and timed to fit with the preset cartoon sequence. But to an audience unused to the new technology of animated film, the presentation fostered a fascinating illusion of life and consciousness. As the showman, stylishly dressed in his dark tuxedo, conducted his interaction with the friendly creature, orchestral sounds from a hidden phonograph created additional atmosphere. McCay's performances must have taken on something of a surrealist quality.

Change of scene: It is the early 1960s, and a leading U.S. computer scientist has been working on a computer program that can print responses to comments and questions typed by any user. He has just completed a prototype designed to simulate the responses of a therapist faced with a new client. He asks his secretary if she would like to try the system and watches carefully as she begins her "consultation." After a little while the secretary seems to become uneasy and asks her boss to leave the room, explaining that she wants to be alone with the therapist.

Over the next few months similar trials with other people showed that many were powerfully influenced by the computer presence indicated by the reactions of the program. They seemed to regard the machine as more than just another piece of gadgetry and reacted to it almost as if it were a living person, conscious, intelligent, and interested in their problems. They confided personal secrets to the machine. Confronted with a profusion of such responses, the computer scientist in question, Joseph Weizenbaum, radically altered his attitude to personal programs. His initial enthusiasm turned to anxiety and disgust as he came to realize what he had helped to unleash, and by the late 1970s he had become outspoken in condemning any application of technology that can produce such direct emotional effects.

What do these two illustrations have in common? Firstly, they show how people become fascinated and involved with physical objects and displays that simulate aspects of life and character. And secondly, they demonstrate how human ingenuity strives to devise artifacts that produce such an involvement. In the chapters that follow, we will explore the nature of the fascination and review attempts to construct objects that, in their psychological impact, transcend their true physical nature.

From the earliest literature to contemporary science fiction there has been a strong tradition of stories about statues, effigies, and robots that simulate living people, and for many centuries artists, engineers, and entertainers have constructed dolls, machines, and dummies that imitate the human figure, human life, and human personality. The pursuit of realism has taxed the resources of ingenuity and of the available technology, and implicit in these efforts has been the dream that one day some means will be found to simulate a human being with a stunning realism.

That day is now drawing near. We live in a world in which vast new horizons are opening up as a result of advances in microtechnology. There are already computers that speak, computers that understand words spoken by humans, and computers that are programmed to portray a vivid "personality" and to "converse" in a "friendly" way. We are thus presented with the possibility of a system that could, to a degree, counterfeit a person. Computers and robots might be programmed with responses that are carefully designed to convey presence and that invite people to interact with them socially. That age-old fascination with the simulation of human characteristics now promises—or threatens—to produce powerful results. The innocent delight that some*thing* can be almost human may now lead to intense social relationships between people and machines.

Such attachments need not involve the sophisticated humanoids occasionally encountered in the pages of science fiction. It will be many, many years before such "creatures" walk our streets. As we shall see, people react emotionally to much cruder devices, and the total simulation of human performance is not by any means a necessary prerequisite for the establishment of a "meaningful relationship." People seem quite ready to tell their troubles to a computer, despite its metal sheen and flashing lights. They may make friends with the machine, finding it sympathetic and accepting it as a social being. Sometimes, indeed, they are so bewildered by its intelligent and humanlike performance that they remain convinced that the responses must be directly controlled by some hidden human agent.

There is, of course, nothing strange or novel about the idea that a person can feel a strong attachment toward something that is not human. Many people would insist that their pet is almost human despite its behavioral limitations and its manifestly nonhuman appearance. And the importance for human beings of such relationships is not to be underestimated either. A pet may be a constant source of comfort and companionship, and the depth of feeling experienced after the death of such an animal may be one of profound bereavement.

The question that now emerges is whether some totally artificial system, some microelectronic device, might not come to elicit similar levels of feeling. Is there some insurmountable barrier preventing the production of acceptable endearing devices, companion artifacts constructed on an assembly line? In some respects such machines might be considerably more attractive than traditional pets, with an ability to converse (and play chess!). It certainly seems feasible to design an artificial system that would afford considerably more "social contact" than a parakeet.

Without a doubt, the picture that emerges from such speculation will alarm many people. The notion of a doting owner lavishing love and devotion on a mere machine is likely to be a cause for concern. A device that could converse amiably and "come to know" us might be seen as endangering the unique quality of human interaction and posing a threat to human relationships. Wouldn't such an upgrading of the talents of a machine decrease the extent to which we prize our contact with other people?

But before such questions can be seriously discussed we need to know more about the feasibility of "intimate" person–machine relationships. At first sight the whole idea might seem preposterous, absurd. Only when we have carefully examined the evidence concerning the relevant technical possibilities and the psychological tendency to become involved with realistic and endearing physical objects can we assess the prospects for such relationships.

One of the central aims of scientists researching in the field of "artificial intelligence" is the simulation of human skills and human personality. Their serious-minded efforts are likely to yield important advances in thinking machines that are "aware" and "in contact with" the world. Meanwhile robotologists are busy designing clever devices that will move, work and live in the world. We can envisage thousands of practical uses for such machines in industry and in the home, but we are likely to overlook a major aspect of their future impact if we regard them principally as devices for welding or for washing dishes. Those developments that will allow machines to deal intelligently and knowledgeably with the world will also promote their "social" skills. We may prefer to regard our mechanical helpers as companions rather than as slaves.

Functional aspects of the new technology are currently receiving unparalleled attention—an understandable state of affairs as long as that technology is likely to remain behind the scenes. But such a state cannot persist for long. Computers are "coming out." They are about to enter our homes and leisure centers, our shops and clinics. We are about to meet the machines. The result of this may be more powerful than we have bargained for. Human beings are inclined toward an animistic perception of the world. That is to say, they have a strong tendency to relate personally to certain objects and to treat them as if they were living creatures. Conditioned by this tendency, the impact of the cleverly programmed "friendly" machine might be overwhelming, for these imminent artifacts that will employ computer technology to simulate character will be socially more powerful than any previous construction. The conclusion that "it almost lives" may be inescapable. We are thus about to encounter engrossing artificial systems that will invite us to enter a fiction: the fiction that they are people with personalities and feelings. On the present evidence there is every indication that many people will readily accept this fiction and will accept as companions devices programmed to behave in ways that belie their nature as mere machines.

PART ONE

FUTURE FRIENDS

CHAPTER 1

The Computer: A Personal Introduction

Models of People and Models of Computers

If we asked some of our friends what a book is, we would receive a number of answers. One person might say "a series of printed pages," another "something you are likely to find in a library," and a third "a stream of an author's thoughts or imaginings." All of these answers are valid in some respect, and they are not incompatible, but they are clearly very different. We would probably be faced with a similar variety of responses if we were to ask what a person is or if we were to ask the same question about a computer. Some of the alternative descriptions stem from radically different models or images held about the object, and the adoption of one model or another can have important consequences.

In psychology we ask what a person is, and recently it has become increasingly more apparent that different psychologists hold very different models that are closely related to the problems that are chosen for study and the methods by which these are examined. For example, the psychologist interested in the processes by which the human brain handles information from the environment often adopts the convenient strategy of maintaining that the individual is rather like a computer. Such a psychologist would speak of "information flow," "memory stores," "processing," and "information retrieval." This computer model has in many ways been very useful, and considerable advances have been made by following the research strategy that assumes that people are little more than information processing machines.

Other psychologists have adopted an alternative model in which the individual is regarded as an animal and placed firmly in the biological and evolutionary context. Psychologists who use this model tend to draw heavily on experiments with other species and stress the part that biological processes and genetic predispositions play in determining the individual's behavior. Others, again, (and this doesn't by any means exhaust the possible list) choose the person model and emphasize those aspects that make the individual a social being. They tend to concentrate, therefore, on the context of social interaction; they deal with such factors as self-image and empathy, and they examine personal feelings and attitudes in great detail.

These different models or images are not directly opposed to one another (the individual *is* a biological creature, and *is* an information processor, and *is* a "person" in the social world—all at the same time) but they certainly provide very different emphases and points of interest. One model may be more appropriate for dealing with one problem than another. If, for example, we want to study the way in which hormones affect mood, then the biological model might seem the most sensible one to adopt. If we want to study the processes of short-term memory, then the computer analogy model might be the most appropriate, and if we want to study someone's personal life-goals, then we would probably adopt the whole person image.

The situation is rather similar in computer science. Many different images or models of the computer are possible. We can regard the computer as a construction of electronic components, as the technologist would; as a fast and powerful number cruncher, as the scientific computer user would; as an elaborate filing system, as the business person would; or as a knowledge processor, as would many contemporary computer scientists and people in the field of artificial intelligence. We can also suggest a new image in which the computer is considered as a social being, a creature or quasi-person. Such an image is already a popular one in science fiction, but because of the way in which most computers are designed and used today, this approach does not yet have much currency in the real world. Changes that are now imminent, however, are likely to alter this state of affairs, at least with regard to certain types of specialized machines.

Again, these different images of the computer are not necessarily incompatible. Whatever image we choose, whether it is number cruncher, knowledge processor, or companion, we would not wish to deny that computers are made from electronic components. In the same way, those psychologists who choose to regard the individual as a social being are not denying that people are made of neurons, muscles, and other such "components." So we don't need to deny the importance of the underlying physical characteristics—the hardware—in order to adopt an image that relies more on the functioning or social significance of a machine or a person.

When considering computers, a distinction must be made between the machine itself—the physical hardware—and the programs that control its operation—the software. Some computers are dedicated to a particular use, and the software never changes (an example of this would be the arcade Space Invaders machine), but most computers will accept a wide variety of legitimate programs, and when a new program is loaded the computer virtually becomes a different machine. We can be playing chess at one time, checking our household accounts at another, and learning French at another, and all with the same machine. Even the basic reactions of the computer can be changed when a new program is loaded. For example, my computer normally prints a "4" on the screen when I press the "4" key, but if I have loaded the Invaders program, then pressing the "4" has the very different effect of moving my "Cosmic Gun" to the left, and the letter "A" now launches a missile. The computer is therefore much more flexible, even in its keyboard action, than the typewriter, which it might superficially resemble.

Programs are easy to write and develop, and the range of possibilities is therefore very great indeed. Once developed, they can be "saved" for future use and also copied any number of times. Software is therefore not only very flexible, but, once developed, it is also very cheap. Within the capacity of the machine an enormous range of software can be loaded at different times, and the same machine can therefore be used to calculate, play cosmic games, play chess, compose music, control garage doors, suggest recipes for meals, or hold "conversations." As such applications become more familiar we can expect the now-dominant model of computer-as-calculator to change, and with the wider introduction of "social interactional" programs we can expect the computer-as-companion model to gain prevalence. Before discussing how computers work, and what it is that gives them their enormous potential as social agents, we will first consider the way in which they have developed through history. As we shall see, this evolution has been marked by a notable growth not only in the power of the machine but also in the range of uses to which it can be applied.

Ancestral Devices

Depending on our precise definition of the term, the history of the computer can be said to span anything from forty to five thousand years. Most accounts usually start with some mention of artificial aids to counting and calculation such as rows of pebbles, knots in dried rushes, and beads on rods. This tends to support, right from the start, the image of computer-as-calculator. If we were to deliberately adopt an alternative model then we might trace a quite different early history, but it is true that in terms of mechanical aids to thinking the mathematical area seems to have had precedence. Paintings and pictograms were also aids to thought, but they did not, of course, involve any form of mechanism. Until recently, the evolution of•machines as intellectual aids continued to be dominated by devices for calculation, and it is only over the last few decades that computers have come to have important non-numerical functions.

Early examples of counting devices have been excavated in the Middle East and date from 3,000 B.C., but the bead and string abacus was not perfected until one thousand years ago. This development, in Japan and China, was paralleled by that of a similar calculating device found in Arabia and introduced into Europe by Gerbert. There were a number of medieval attempts to produce alternative calculating mechanisms, and during this period Ramon Lüll built his *Ars Magna,* a contraption that manipulated symbols rather than numbers and that was used to make predictions according to a system that seems to have included elements of astrology, logic, and the tarot.

Lüll's machine may have fired the imagination of many of his contemporaries, but the practical usefulness of the information which it generated was negligible. Mechanical arithmetic devices, however, were useful, and effort was continually exerted to find new ways to extend and improve them. At the beginning of the seventeenth century the Scottish aristocrat John Napier invented logarithms, which simplified the processes of multiplication and division, and he mechanized their use by means of calculating rods. A few years later the logarithmic slide-rule was constructed by the British mathematician William Oughtred, and in France in 1642 the nineteen-year-old Blaise Pascal invented an adding machine that incorporated geared wheels representing hundreds, tens, and units. If five twos were added in succession, for example, the "unit" wheel would automatically return to zero and the "tens" wheel would register a "one." Soon after this another philosopher, Gottfried Leibniz, built a somewhat superior machine that could multiply, divide, and extract square roots. Machines that involved variations of the geared-wheels theme were to be found in offices and laboratories until comparatively recently. However, these heavy, cumbersome, expensive, and noisy machines quickly became consigned to the junkyard with the advent of the electronic calculator. Few machine species could ever have become extinct so rapidly.

The calculators of Pascal and Leibniz were, both in their conception and their operation, very different from today's computers, since each step in a calculation had to be controlled entirely by the operator. Thus, the next stage of development centered upon the automation of procedures so that a series of functions could be carried out by the machine itself. Such an instrument was first devised by the British genius Charles Babbage. He was a man of many interests and many achievements. Having invented the locomotive cow-catcher, the ophthalmo-scope, and the speedometer, he was the first to perform the calculations necessary for drawing up reliable actu-arial tables of the type used in insurance. For the fifty years before his death in 1871, however, his major pre-occupation was the design of automatic calculating machines.

Babbage's basic idea was that a machine could be constructed of gears and levers that would operate under the control of punched cards, storing intermediate an-swers for later computation and finally printing the result. He designed two elaborate machines. The first of these, the Difference Engine, was constructed of finely worked metal cams and gears and was used to calculate precise astronomical tables for navigational use. The more ambitious Analytical Engine was not built during Babbage's lifetime—it was beyond the scope of contemporary metalwork technology—but its design incorporated several important elements that were later to become essential features of electronic computers.

The Analytical Engine was to have been steam driven, with a memory that could hold a thousand fifty-digit numbers. Apart from this mechanical memory, or "store," it was to have a "mill" to perform the arithmetical operations (this is equivalent to what is today called a logic unit) and "sequence mechanisms" to supervise the order of operations (today such functions are carried out by a control unit and by the program). Babbage also proposed that the information should be entered into the machine in the form of punched cards like those then in use in advanced weaving looms, and again this anticipated future developments in the operation of electronic machines. Babbage's collaborator on many of his projects was Ada Augusta, Lady Lovelace, herself an accomplished mathematician. She once commented that ". . . the Analytical Engine weaves algebraic patterns just as the Jacquard loom weaves flowers and leaves."

Lady Lovelace also discussed the machine's potential and its limitations and attempted to correct what she felt to be general misapprehensions about the Engine's capabilities. In particular she maintained that because it was a machine the Engine could only follow a preset pattern of operations and could never originate anything of itself: ". . . it has no power of anticipating any analytical relations or truths. Its province is to assist us in making available what we are already acquainted with." Today, when many computer scientists want to claim that computers *can* be original and that their action is *not* wholly predictable from the program, those who insist that machines can act only in strict accordance with instructions are said to be voicing "Lady Lovelace's Objection."

Babbage was a very eccentric individual. In his later years, for example, he led an intense campaign against organ-grinders and other street musicians. He felt that he had enough problems on his hands without being plagued by a racket outside his window! The construction of the second Engine presented great difficulties, and his failure to produce a working model eventually led to the withdrawal of financial support by the British government. An attempt, with Lady Lovelace, to apply mathematical formulae to win money at horse racing also failed to raise the necessary funds. With hindsight, it is now realized that Babbage's lack of success at the practical level was simply due to a lack of technological backup. As in the case of so many early inventors, his ideas called for engineering contributions that were simply not available at the time. Many of his highly innovative suggestions, however, foreshadowed later developments, and for this reason Babbage now occupies an honored place in the history of technology and is often credited with having invented the computer.

The next important development in the story concerns a peripheral element—the input mechanism—and it illustrates how necessity is often the mother of invention. The United States Census Bureau collected so much data in their 1880 census that they had severe difficulties in processing it. The answer to the problem was supplied by Herman Hollerith with a design for a fast punched-card data system. Questionnaire responses were punched as holes in various positions on cards, and when these were fed through a counting machine electrical contact was made by a wire "brush" whenever a hole was present. The rapid feeding of a deck of such cards through the machine greatly speeded up the process of tabulating the census results, and Hollerith's answer to this specific problem generated a system with many other possible applications. He had developed a method of feeding masses of data quickly and reliably into a machine.

Hollerith set up a company to market this and other business equipment and thereby founded a corporation that was later to become IBM. His original census machine was not really a calculator but a highly efficient counting mechanism. The company diversified its interests into many aspects of the business systems field and was to benefit greatly from a considerable growth in the market for mechanical calculators. Some other companies specialized in more sophisticated machines for scientific use, and there was even renewed interest in the possibility of a "logic machine."

From the middle of the nineteenth century a number of "logical algebras" had been devised. Symbols were made to stand for statements, and rules were devised for determining how such symbols could be manipulated. Initially such systems were based entirely on traditional logical principles, but innovations were later introduced to explore the consequences of alternative sets of logical conventions. This "mechanical" approach to rational thinking clearly lent itself to machine application, and the American philosopher Charles Pierce, who had himself created a number of logical algebras, drew up plans for a logic machine that was then built by one of his students.

With advances in electronics and electrical engineering, it became clear that the mechanical calculator would give way to a new generation of machines in which computation would be achieved by electrical switches and electric currents rather than by moving wheels and levers. During the 1930s a number of advanced electromechanical calculators were designed. Many of the earliest applications of these machines were military, involving, for example, the calculation of missile trajectories for ballistics research. Their capability in these areas proved so valuable that several further projects received generous aid from the U.S. government. One of these was based at Harvard and resulted in the first apparatus that can, without qualification, be called a computer. This machine, the Harvard Mark I, was completed in 1944 by IBM working with Howard Aiken, who was later to refer to it as "Babbage's dream come true."

The Second World War saw further advances in the field of electronics, largely as a result of research into radar, and these developments made the construction of a totally electronic computer feasible. The first of these, the Electronic Numerical Integrator and Calculator (mercifully known as ENIAC), was built in 1945. This Leviathan weighed thirty tons and included 18,000 thermionic tubes. The heat generated by its operation was equivalent to that of about 100 one-kilowatt electric fires, and a good deal of time was spent changing burned-out tubes and maintaining the circuits. When it was operating, though, it was impressive. As with so many of the early computers, it was designed as a general-purpose calculator, but the first problems it tackled were almost all of military significance. ENIAC's first major task involved calculations for the Manhattan Project, which developed the first atomic bomb.

Because ENIAC was entirely electronic it was very fast, some 800 times as fast as Harvard Mark I. Speed is vitally important for most computer applications, and this aspect of the technology has been developed to such an extent that by today's standards even ENIAC seems sluggish. Nevertheless, the work it could cope with was phenomenal by the standards of the period, and it was felt that just a few machines of this type would be able to cope with all the major computational needs of the entire United States. IBM at this time suggested that perhaps four such machines would suffice for this purpose. That estimate proved to be rather misleading. Current figures suggest that by 1984 there will be six million computers in the U.S.! But not everybody was so limited in their vision of the computer future, and one man who fully realized the potential of such machines was a mathematician named John von Neumann. He had made important contributions to theoretical physics and had established a new branch of mathematics—"games theory"—before turning his attention to the development of computers. In 1945 he designed EDVAC—the Electronic Discrete Variable Automatic Calculator. This used a system for representing both instructions and data in terms of a series of on-off switches and was the first machine in which both the data and the program itself could be stored in the computer memory. In many ways EDVAC embodied most of the essentials of modern computer design. By current standards it was a primitive machine, and yet it marked a major step toward computers as they are today; this is, therefore, a good point at which to describe the basic "architecture" of modern computers.

How Computers Work

A computer is a very flexible machine. It combines features of a calculator, a filing system, a translator, a dictionary, and a stopwatch. A program instructs the machine how to use its various basic functions to perform the desired task, and, since many quite different programs can be executed, the computer, unlike the refrigerator or alarm clock, is not restricted to performing one basic task but can be regarded as a multipurpose machine.

A computer interacts with the world around it, taking in information, processing it, and then presenting results to a human operator. Our special interest is how the flexibility may be harnessed and shaped so that the machine can generate a "social presence." To understand how this is possible it is helpful to understand something of the basic operation of the computer. If we are able to demystify the machine, then we will be able to understand how complex "social" tasks may be achieved as a result of the highly organized activity of barely perceptible electric currents passing through microscopic circuitry.

Computers accept data, or *input*. They process this and then produce results, or *output*. The processing of data follows a sequence of operations determined by the *program* with which the machine is loaded. Within the machine there are the equivalent of thousands or even millions of components, and they are organized as a series of functional stages, the overall design of these being known as the "computer architecture."

A *memory* holds the original data, the outcome of any intermediate calculations and the final results. The particular numbers or facts that are stored at any time will depend upon the data and the program being used, and when the work has been completed this information is then erased from the memory. There is, however, another type of memory in which a set of permanent "reference" facts are stored. The contents of this sort of memory are never changed and are always accessible.

The various arithmetical and logical operations that are called for during the execution of a program are performed within an *arithmetic logic unit,* and the sequence of the operations is governed by a *control unit.* This moves information from the store to the arithmetic logic unit and back again, and the step-by-step processing of the information is paced by a *clock.* The overall speed (and therefore to some extent the power) of the machine is determined by the rhythm of this clock, and in a modern computer it may beat many thousands or even millions of times every second.

An *input control* center receives the instructions and data that are fed into the machine and translates them into a form that other parts of the computer can easily handle. The *output control* center transforms the patterns of electronic impulses which emerge from processing and directs this decoded information out to an external device to be stored or read by a human operator. Input into the machine may be via a special typewriter or keyboard, punched paper or cards, or magnetic tape or disk. The computer also directs its output to one of these devices or to a television-like screen (sometimes known as the "video display monitor").

It has long been a dream that one day a machine might "speak" and "hear," and some systems now under development do have provision for human speech input and synthesized voice output. There are formidable problems involved in such projects, but considerable progress has already been made, and the current profusion of research directed toward both voice recognition and speech production leads many experts to the conclusion that acceptable levels of performance will be achieved within a few years. Computer speech and hearing clearly have a particular relevance for applications designed to exploit the animistic response, and they will be described in some detail in a later chapter.

So far we have gone only part of the way toward demystifying the computer. The gross structure of the machine, described in terms of its functional architecture, makes it clear that input is translated, processed, and then retranslated into output, but we have to consider the functioning at a microscopic level if we want to see how it is possible for a machine to calculate and operate "logically." An explanation of how logical and mathematical processes can be represented by the functioning of electronic circuitry will enable us to see why the computer is so flexible and will help us to appreciate that even highly complex aspects of human social performance may be reduced to a form in which they are capable of simulation by a machine.

Perhaps the most illuminating aspect of the relationship between logical systems and their electronic representation is the fact that any number, symbol, or word can be translated into an on-off pattern of signals or electrical pulses. In the type of computer with which we are concerned (this is a "digital" computer; there are also "analogue" computers, but we need not discuss them here), a pulse, or "charge," may be "present" or "absent" —there is no "in-between" state. If, by analogy, we imagine a row of, say, eight flashlights, each of which may be independently switched on or off, then it is clear that many unique overall patterns are possible (in fact 256). If we were to arrange with another person a set of "translation rules" for assigning a meaning to each individual pattern of lights, then we could communicate any one of 256 prearranged messages with just a single display.

Given a sequence of such displays we could convey a very complex message. It takes only twenty-six different patterns to represent the letters of the alphabet (five flashlights would be sufficient), and so, using a succession of displays, any text, even the complete works of Shakespeare, could be transmitted. Special patterns would need to be assigned to punctuation marks and the like, but that does not present a problem. If we were to keep pace with a preset rhythm we could also perform the same trick using a single flashlight. A pattern of "ons" and "offs" within eight time-periods would now be equivalent to the eight flashlights in a row. We would merely be substituting a temporal pattern for a spatial one.

The transmission of verbal and numerical messages in such a manner is hardly a new one. The Morse Code operates in roughly the same way and has been used to send telegraph messages since 1844. The Code is effective because the operator who receives the message uses the same translation rules as the one who sends it. The computer also works by applying such a code. When we press the letter "B" or the number "9" on a computer keyboard the machine translates this into an "on-off" sequence. It uses these patterns during its operation and then conveniently translates the information back into letters or numbers at the end of the task.

An "on" signal is generally represented in printed texts as "1" and "off" as "0." The system of encoding numbers and messages in this way is known as the "binary system" and a single element (a "1" or a "0") is known as a "bit," which is short for "binary digit." (A byte is a collection of bits, generally eight.) Bits of information are used by the machine in the performance of calculations and logical operations, and they can also be stored in memory as magnetic states. All numbers, symbols, or words can therefore be stored and processed in the form of a sequence or pattern of bits.

The next fundamental principle is that any problem that can be precisely defined can be reduced to a logical form. The computer is a machine that is specifically constructed to deal with logical processes, and it can therefore handle, at least in principle, any problem or task that can be clearly specified. The qualification "in principle" is very important here, and "dealing with" or "handling" a problem is not the same as solving it. Nevertheless, the principle suggests that the potential scope of the computer is very wide indeed.

Some of the most important statements about the nature of computing and computers were made by philosophers, dealing with theories of mathematics and formal logic, before such machines had actually been built. In the nineteenth century the logician George Boole showed that certain operations in logic are absolutely fundamental and that they combine in a systematic and lawful fashion. Boole played an important role in the quest to show that all mathematics could ultimately be reduced to logic, and in the 1930s the British mathematician Alan Turing was able to show that, using data in binary form, any mathematical task can in principle be performed with just three logical operations—"AND," "NOT," and "OR."

The functional heart of computer circuitry consists of electrical switches that perform just such logical operations, and particular switch arrangements can therefore represent logical forms. A specified task, no matter what its source or content, can be formalized as a logical construction, and this can then be reduced to a pattern of switch settings within the electronic circuitry. The information is processed by the flow of current, and the resulting pattern of electrical impulses is then reconstructed as meaningful output.

In this way highly complex tasks are reduced to a sequence of elementary operations. These are organized meticulously by the machine and are orchestrated so efficiently that the most intricate of tasks may be performed very rapidly. At this level the machine works automatically, but the general plan for the job is of course dictated by the list of instructions that constitutes the program. Any term within a program undergoes a reduction to binary form and ultimately ends up as a sequence of electrical switch settings.

Programming

A program instructs the machine to carry out a sequence of operations. It may tell the computer, for example, to calculate the square root of 12, to add this to a number that has previously been computed, and then to test whether the sum is greater than 50. It could instruct the machine to print "YES" if the number did exceed 50 and "NO" if it didn't. Programs are lists of statements that instruct the computer in a step-by-step way about the operations necessary to complete the task. The programmer therefore has to have a clear idea of the nature of the problem and the operations necessary for solving it.

The earliest computers were presented with instructions and data directly in binary form. This made things relatively easy for the machine but was of course very laborious for the operator, and so later developments were dedicated to ensuring that an increasing percentage of the work was handed over to the machine. Modern computers now accept instructions in the form of words and symbols that are easier to use, and the machine then translates these for itself. The programmer must be familiar with certain "key words" that have a special significance for the machine, and he or she must also follow a strict set of rules in writing the program. The set of rules and conventions that the programmer must follow comprises a programming *language*. There are an increasing number of computer languages, with names like FORTRAN, ALGOL, COBOL, and PASCAL, which tend to get adopted for specific types of application, as their various strengths and weaknesses become known.

The machine is preset to receive instructions in a particular language. When an appropriate program is loaded into the computer it is automatically translated into binary form. The programmer needs to have a detailed knowledge of the language but does not need to know much about the machine. The skills required of the programmer are therefore quite different from those of the computer technologist, and programmers may be quite disdainful of the machine. Aaron Sloman, a writer on Artificial Intelligence, may have been reflecting the opinion of many programmers when he described computers as "those ugly boxes with mysterious noises and flashing lights." The task of programming involves skills of problem-solving and composition and the formulation of strategies tailor-made to particular objectives. It is primarily a pen-and-paper exercise, and it might be considered largely irrelevant that the end-product is to be implemented on a machine.

A program consists of a sequence of instructions, written as separate "lines" that are numbered in a definite order. A line will often carry an instruction for the machine to return to a previous line or to redo a whole section, and so the computer may make skips and loops and backward jumps, and the progression is generally more like a dance than a sprint. It is relatively easy to make a mistake and send the machine into an endless metaphorical spin or to have it stop at the wrong place. The process of identifying and correcting such mistakes is known as "debugging" the program.

Some programming languages are rather difficult to learn, but there are now several that have been designed to be acquired (at least at an elementary level) in just a few hours. One such is BASIC (Beginner's All-purpose Symbolic Instruction Code), which was devised at Dartmouth College in the late 1960s. Using this language we can illustrate the type of format and instructions that a program is likely to include. Here is a line from a BASIC program:

10 INPUT X: INPUT A$

The "10" here is merely a line number. It is a label that can be referred to in later lines. The line numbers don't need to start at "1," and it is good programming practice to leave "spaces" ("10," for example, might be followed by "25") in case we want to insert an additional line (say "15") later. "INPUT" is a key word that the machine will "recognize," and it tells the computer to accept data from an external source (a keyboard terminal, for example). The first INPUT statement means "accept a number and call it 'X'." If, when the machine waits for "X," we type in "52," then the value of "X" will become 52, so that if a later instruction tells the machine to print "X + 10" it will then print "62."

The second part of the line is also an INPUT instruction, but because of the $ sign the machine will treat the input not as a number but as a string of symbols—letters, figures, words, or sentences. Whatever we type in at this stage will be labeled "A$" ("'A' string"), and if later in the program we have the line:

20 PRINT A$

then the text that we have entered will be printed on to the visual display unit or on to a teletype.

The program can also contain its own text. When the line:

30 PRINT "HELLO"

is executed, then "HELLO" will appear on the screen. It is important to realize that *any* text at all can be inserted between quotation marks. We can therefore make the computer "say" anything we want. Any quip, complaint, endearment, or obscenity can be printed by the machine and, if the output is to a speech synthesizer, spoken by it.

In considering the social potential of computers, the most interesting programs are those that structure an interaction between a person and the machine. Here is a very simple example:

10 PRINT "WHAT'S YOUR NAME?": INPUT B$

20 PRINT "THANK YOU," B$ ",I'M DELIGHTED TO MEET YOU"

In executing this program the machine will accept any name the operator types in and will then greet him or her "personally." The computer will first print:

WHAT'S YOUR NAME?

and will then wait until the operator types in text. This will be treated as "B string," and when a "return" key is pressed, indicating the end of the string, the computer will move on to line 20. If the operator has typed in "PETER," then the output of the machine will read:

THANK YOU, PETER, I'M DELIGHTED TO MEET YOU.

If we wanted the machine to be more "friendly," then it could be programmed to recognize certain common names and to print out a more familiar form (thus "PETER" might become "PETE"). It would achieve this by recognizing the name and simply amending the text of the string. We could allow our program to do this by adding lines into the sequence before the output statement:

15 IF B\$ = "PETER" THEN LET B\$ = "PETE"

17 IF B\$ = "ELIZABETH" THEN LET B\$ = "LIZ"

Now if a Peter or an Elizabeth should encounter the program they are in for a surprise, though a John or a Susan would be unaffected. Quite startling reactions can be produced even by simple tricks such as this one, and this theme—the pronounced psychological reaction to simple programming strategies—is one to which we will return later.

The "IF . . . THEN" convention found in lines 15 and 17 may be used very powerfully in a program. "IF" and "THEN" are key words that are instantly recognized by the machine as having a special function. "IF . . . THEN" is not only used to alter text, as in the example, but can be used to conditionally set numerical values and to "branch" programs. Suppose we have written a program in two sections, one designed to interact with children and the other to interact with adults. We could begin the program by asking the person's age and, depending on whether this was greater than, say, 14, we could "GOTO" the beginning of one section or the other. Here is an example of such a program (the arithmetical symbol < means "less than"):

50 PRINT "HOW OLD ARE YOU?" : INPUT X

60 IF X < 14 GO TO 100

70 PRINT "I LIKE ADULTS LIKE YOU"

80 END

100 PRINT "I LIKE CHILDREN LIKE YOU"

110 END

Here the machine waits at line 50 until the person enters the age and then goes on to line 60 to test whether this is less than 14. If it is less, then the computer skips to line 100, prints its message, and ends at 110. If the age is *not* less than 14, however, the machine simply goes on to the next line, 70, and after printing "I LIKE ADULTS LIKE YOU" it ends at line 80.

We saw in the case of the Peter and Elizabeth program how string text, as well as numbers, could be tested in an "IF . . . THEN" statement. In branching programs such as those used to conduct medical interviews with patients, the machine frequently tests whether the answer to a question is "YES" or "NO" and, depending on the answer, probes further or skips to the next topic.

Even quite a short program can generate a good deal of output. If we introduce a "loop" into the program, we can make the machine perform the same routine again and again. This is best illustrated with a simple mathematical example:

15 FOR X = 1 TO 100000 : PRINT X, X ↑ 2
20 NEXT X
30 END

The "FOR . . . NEXT" convention is another that is immediately recognized by the machine, and it is used in this program to set up a loop between lines 15 and 20. On each circuit of the loop the value of X is automatically increased by one, and each time we get a numerical print-out of the square (that is, "X multiplied by X"). The "square of X" in BASIC is "X ↑ 2," the cube is "X ↑ 3," and so on. The end product of this program would therefore be a table of squares from 1 to 100,000. This upper limit has been set in line 15, and when X reaches this value the machine leaves the loop and stops at line 30.

Even with the simple examples provided here, we begin to get some idea of the power that programs may have. There are many special terms and operations besides those that have been introduced, and by using various combinations very complex structures can be produced. It is not uncommon for a program to contain hundreds of lines, and it may involve such sequence gymnastics as a loop within a loop within a loop. Some programs are written to modify themselves as they are used, and they may be said to "grow" or "learn from experience." For this reason the outcome of a program is not always predictable, but an element of unpredictability can be built in much more directly by using the "random function"—"RND" in BASIC.

The following program provides an illustration of this:

```
10 x = RND (1) : IF x <.33 GOTO 100
20 PRINT "I'M FEELING HAPPY" : GOTO 10
100 PRINT "I'M FEELING SAD" : GOTO 10
```

This program would lead the machine to produce an unending succession of "happy" and "sad" statements. The first part of line 10 sets X to some random value between 0 and 1 (such as .57 or .27) and the second part tests whether this is less than .33. If it is less, then the machine skips to line 100 and prints the "sad" statement. Otherwise it prints the "happy" statement. In either case it returns afterward to set another value for X and continues as before. Because of the test-value set for X (.33) this program would produce, overall, one-third "sad" statements and two-thirds "happy" statements. With a few extra well-chosen lines we could introduce additional statements and include some random timing procedure, so that different feeling statements would be liable to pop up at odd moments. The random selection of a preset vocabulary lies at the heart of some simple programs for poetry writing, although much more complex strategies will be involved if the poems are to be well-structured and meaningful.

We have thus examined some of the basic elements of programming—the recognition of strings, random functions, loops, and conditional ("IF . . . THEN") instructions. We can see how these might be combined to make a program not only useful but also interesting in the content and style of its output. With imagination, even the novice programmer can produce a program that is full of "human interest," because the success of such a composition depends at least as much upon social and literary skills as upon technical know-how.

The examples used have deliberately been related to interaction and communication rather than computation, in line with our general interest in the potential of the computer as a companion machine. They provide little idea of what might be achieved with sophisticated programs, but it is remarkable how even simple strategies and tricks can produce marked reactions from the user. This is an important phenomenon. People seem ready to be impressed by what the machine can do. They smile when it uses their name, they laugh when it makes some typically human comment. Even more important is the fact that they often seem to treat the computer as if it were some kind of living creature.

The Plastic Machine

Computers are staggeringly flexible. They have numerous functions and can be programmed to perform an enormous variety of tasks. They can produce music, write poems, solve problems in geometry, or cast horoscopes. They can match partners for dates, diagnose diseases, or teach spelling. They can play chess, store a vast number of names and addresses, or help to animate cartoons. For each of these special applications they must be appropriately programmed, and for some of them they must be equipped with extra output devices. The heart of each operation, however, is always the sequential processing of information, and this is achieved by the flow of electrons through electronic circuitry.

For the people who generally use the machines, however, it would be a mistake to concentrate too heavily on the technicalities—after all, when we look at a painting, we do not need to know the chemical constituents of the paint. Such knowledge might be of some interest in its own right, but it would probably detract from an appreciation of the work of art. Similarly, a computer user who strives to maintain an electron-flow perspective is likely to be distracted from concentrating on practical applications and the interactive potential of the machine. It is better to see the machine in terms of what it *can do* rather than of *how* it does it.

When we meet a friend, few of us have in mind the underlying physiology that allows the other person to react to us. We do not imagine the nerve-cells firing in the brain or the muscles pulling at the bones of the hand we are shaking. It's not that we would deny these aspects; we simply choose to view our social contact as a person rather than as a physiological entity. In the same way, when interacting with a computer, we might choose to ignore the underlying electronic realities and treat the machine as if it were something other than a piece of technical gadgetry.

Even if we agree with this, some of the possible alternative images would seem to be more acceptable than others. In particular, the proposition that a computer might be treated as if it were another person is at first sight outrageous. Evidence suggests, however, that people are rather prone to adopting such an anthropomorphic view and that certain features of the hardware and software can encourage this type of response. How is it, then, that a machine that is basically designed as a piece of apparatus for the performance of arithmetic calculations and logical analyses might eventually become a social intimate? The answer is that the machine is flexible enough and powerful enough to produce a very wide range of stimuli, including many that we normally accept as cues to intelligence, friendliness, good humor, and other characteristically human attributes. Furthermore, such cues may be produced with such selectivity and good timing that a human presence is powerfully conveyed.

A degree of performance may be achieved that we have otherwise experienced only within the context of human interaction. In this way the computer surpasses the limitations built into our conception of a machine, and we must search for an alternative classification. One obvious metaphor presents itself, and as a result we are likely to regard the computer as "more like a person than like a machine." And a program can, of course, be written in such a way that it encourages this view. Computer-based systems are potentially very powerful in their ability to provide cues that are likely to be interpreted as signs of "organism," "life," and "intelligence." Even simple objects are sometimes experienced as if they were living objects. Human beings seem to have a built-in bias toward judging things to be living and humanlike. This tendency is called "animism," and the animistic response is elicited by a wide variety of physical objects. Those features that stimulate animism can be used to enhance the social impact of machine systems, and in addition the cleverly programmed computer can be genuinely reactive to the human user.

Certain severe limitations that operate against the full counterfeiting of human reaction patterns will remain, but these need not prevent social interaction between the person and the machine. Animism always involves going beyond the concrete evidence and making up for the shortcomings of the stimulus. This psychological tendency is likely, therefore, to compensate for technical limitations. When we examine the strength of the animistic responses that can be elicited by very simple stimuli (it has been demonstrated that even moving geometric shapes can suggest life and personality), then some idea of the potential of sophisticated computer systems will be appreciated. The possibilities presented by the new technology represent an entirely new order of pseudo-social cues. Over the centuries many inventive engineers have attempted to construct humanoid automata, and it is exciting—and perhaps disturbing—to think how they might have applied today's technology if it had been available to them. Within a working lifetime such inventors would have been lucky to see one major advance in basic technology. Today we hardly have time to explore the possibilities offered by a revolutionary advance before it is superseded by some new device. Never before has the time-span between laboratory bench and consumer product been so short; never before have so many people had the opportunity to become directly acquainted with "state of the art" technology.

There is still a tendency to think of the computer as a calculator, even though many or even most of the current applications are non-numerical. Even when complex mathematics *is* involved in a program, the resulting output may take the form of a musical passage, a drawing, or a poem. And mathematical solutions have been applied to such nonmathematical problems as deciding whether two literary passages are by the same author or whether a suicide note is fake or real. The computing power that is used to maintain business files, process satellite information, and calculate destructive military potential can also be used in much "softer" applications to write detective stories (as yet not very good ones), play backgammon (better than the current human world champion), or tell jokes to children. Already there have been computer-based attempts to simulate aspects of human personality, and there are a number of programs that provide psychotherapeutic counseling for those with personal problems. By changing the program we can in many respects change the nature of the computer itself, and it is, by virtue of this phenomenon, a "plastic" machine.

It may require a giant step of the imagination to change the image of the computer-as-calculator to one of the computer-as-companion. It does not, however, require vast technical skill to write programs in which some of the characteristics of our human friends are simulated. From now on this is likely to be achieved with more and more success. Many current limitations are likely to be overcome by further technical developments, and our powerful animistic predisposition will continually exert its influence, so that the psychological impact will be greater than that merited by the potential of the machine itself. In later chapters we shall examine the power of animism in other contexts and the ways in which it has been relentlessly exploited in pursuit of the quasihuman object. However, all former successes will pale beside the developments we face in the very near future. As computers are programmed specifically for realistic personal interaction, the animistic response will ensure that they are given new roles as companions and intimates. However disturbing we might initially find such an idea, it now seems quite implausible that such developments will not take place. We will see that it is not difficult to adopt a more social model and to forget the fact that a computer is a mere machine.

CHAPTER 2

New Technology, New Techniques

The past ten years have seen a technology explosion like nothing that has occurred before. This has meant that certain things that were previously impossible are now achieved routinely, and many things that have been possible for some time are now done with greater speed and lower cost. In this chapter we will review some of the incredible changes in technology that have taken place within this period and anticipate some of the developments that are promised for the near future.

Computers have always been fast, but their speed has increased enormously in the past few years and will certainly go on increasing. For many microcompanion applications the phenomenal speed which can now be achieved may not be vitally important, but some problems do involve long and complex analyses of masses of data. Composing a sentence, for example, may require a search through thousands of possible words. Speed also allows the machine to deal with a variety of problems within the time that would normally be needed to deal with just one, and so one very fast machine can do the work of several "normal fast" ones. For commercial work this means that the unit cost of the job to be done is therefore considerably less.

The Chip

Today's microchips pack the equivalent of a hundred thousand transistors and other components into a single tiny (.2-inch square) multilayered sandwich of silicon with ultrathin lines of connecting aluminum printed onto the many surfaces and linking individual elements into a circuit of great complexity. The micro*processor* chip has the whole of the central processing unit of a computer (including the "clock") assembled in the single tiny fragment, and the micro*computer* chip has all this plus memory and some input and output facilities. In terms of equivalence to the moving parts in a conventional telephone exchange, a single chip may be several times as complex as *all* the exchanges in California put together.

Because a microcomputer's components are so closely packed, the conduction time between components—the time it takes the electrical current to flow—is itself very small. All operations within a single processing phase must, of course, be completed before the next "tick" of the processor clock, and so the clock speed determines the overall speed of the machine. The clocks in high-speed machines today "tick" at the rate of about 200 million times a second, but an emergent technology based on the Josephson junction switch will achieve about fifty times that speed!

Another important limiting factor is how many bits of information the computer can process simultaneously. This is known as the "word length." Early micros were limited to four-bit words; eight is the most common figure today, but machines operating on word lengths of thirty-two or even sixty-four bits are already in the pipeline.

Of course, clock speed or word length are not the only factors that determine the overall power of a computer, and the other major factor—memory—has also been the subject of intense technological development in recent years. RAM (Random Access Memory) chips have been developed that can store 4K (4,000) or 8K (8,000) bytes of information, and these can often be added to the machine in module form so that the system is expandable to, say, 64K, thus providing a mass of instantly accessible data. However, this is very limited compared with what appears to be on the horizon. Memories in which information is stored in the form of magnetic "bubbles" will soon offer fast access to several *thousand* K, and there are even plans for a fast memory that will hold 10 million million K—equivalent to a production of three books a day every day for a million years!

At present we have to content ourselves with considerably less, but of course the other type of memory (known as "archival memory"), in which data is called from a longer-term store or "fund" into the working memory, is cheap and unlimited. Ordinary audiocassettes are often used for this purpose, but optical and holographic alternatives based on laser technology are now under active development.

User-Friendliness

These developments in computer power mean that we are unlikely to come across any real power obstacle to the manufacture of the tenable companion machine. There is no danger that we simply won't be able to make powerful enough machines to handle satisfactory interactions at a social level with the human user. A little later we'll consider cost factors and demonstrate that there is, similarly, little likelihood of a cost barrier to the propagation of "plastic pals." But one element that initially seems likely to cause real problems concerns the approachability, or user-friendliness, of the machines. Would people really choose to chat with a machine?

Would they be able to work it, or would the whole operation require a complexity that the average person wouldn't want to bother with?

At present, it's certainly true that computers make considerable demands on users, and, to exploit their potential to the full, a variety of sophisticated pragramming techniques are likely to be required. Interaction inevitably demands a familiarity with operating procedures, but the fact is that machines of any type require some specialized knowledge. Those that make few demands on the user and that can't easily be misused are said to be "idiot-proof." Today's computers may not possess this welcome property, but there is no reason why they shouldn't in the future. Indeed, the flexibility and intelligence of the machine itself should make it the idiot-proof instrument par excellence—provided, of course, that the designers and programmers have this feature in mind and combine imagination with the potential inherent in the technology.

The specialized knowledge required for computing today should not be overestimated. Intelligent eight-year-olds can be found operating machines and writing simple (and not so simple) programs. In the early days of computing, the machine itself did relatively little, and the programmer and operator had a great deal to do. To make any instruction usable by the machine, they had to translate their task through a number of tedious stages into machine acceptable form. Today more and more is done by the machine itself. We have seen how the development of the so-called high-level languages has greatly simplified the programming process. These languages have relatively few rules and conventions, they reflect normal language to a greater degree, and they take little time to learn.

But even this situation is less than perfect when we come to consider that ideal companion machine. While the initial programming might be very complex, the machine would be purchased preprogrammed, so that the user, in interaction with it, would never need to go into programming details. Today many scientists who use computers for calculating statistics, for example, use a package that has been prewritten by programmers. The scientists simply have to name a statistics test they want to use and the package takes over. They need never know the details of the program. Nevertheless, they still have to enter their basic commands and data via a keyboard terminal or on punched cards, and so there is, in a sense, an "unnatural" stage that they have to go through before getting their results. If this, too, were to be circumvented, then truly natural interaction would be achieved, and as a consequence machines would be much more approachable.

As we shall see later, even terminal-based machines permit effective personal interaction, but only to a very limited extent—people do not communicate naturally via terminals. Reading may be a common skill, but typing is alien to most people and is certainly not the ideal medium for social interaction. What progress, then, is being made toward ordinary communication with machines, in the form of their understanding of spoken language and their speech output? This is a key question in the development of optimal machine companions.

Talking with Machines: They Talk to Us

It is considerably easier to develop machines that speak than it is to produce those with the ability to understand us when we speak. This is because "understanding" is a high-level process. "Hearing" by itself is useless for the sort of application we have in mind, whereas "hearing with understanding" is crucial. But if a machine can produce something on a terminal screen, then it doesn't need to understand in order to translate that terminal output, via a voice synthesizer, into spoken form. Thus, what is required is a method by which printed words and phrases can be effectively translated into recognizable sounds.

There are several ways in which this could be done. We could record someone speaking a large "dictionary" of words (each perhaps with several different intonations) and then call them up into sentences as appropriate. Alternatively, we could analyze words into individual sound segments (phonemes) and synthesize them to order. This latter method is the one that has been given the most attention in recent years. The sound is generated by reproducing the wave pattern (or spectrogram) involved. This is generally done by electronically synthesizing signals, although some designers have preferred to use computer-generated instructions to a mechanically operated mouthlike cavity with artificial teeth, lips, and tongue (reminiscent of earlier attempts by automata makers).

The results to date have been very encouraging. Single words are reproduced with clarity, although the overall sound of a complex phrase or sentence often sounds mechanical or robotlike. The intonation pattern appropriate to strings of words occurring naturally in speech requires a degree of analysis that is not easy to achieve. At present, then, there is little danger of confusing the speech of a real person with that of a machine, but the aim of increasing the naturalness of synthetic voices is currently the subject of several research programs. One of the faults of present systems tends to be that they sound rather too formal and unemotional, and they do not include the hesitations, variations, and imperfections contained in natural speech. The voices also seem to be mostly adult, American accented, and male, although these features reflect the apparent preferences of the designers rather than any technical constraints.

There are problems of speech synthesis whatever the level of analysis on which the machine bases its output. If it analyzes part-words, then mispronunciations will be frequent, for English pronunciation is notoriously difficult and unruly (a commonly quoted example is the "ou" component in the words "though," "thought," "through," and "bough"). Yet if the machine analyzes at the whole-word level then it will need a very large "dictionary" in its memory, and even then there are words such as "wind" and "tear" that are pronounced quite differently depending on the meaning. Assessment of meaning comes from considering the context, but if we need the computer to actually *understand* the sentence being spoken in order to accomplish this, then an entirely new realm of complexity is introduced.

Although state-of-the-art voice production is by no means perfect, it might still be adequate for our immediate needs in a companion machine. People would probably learn to tolerate the verbal inadequacies of a mechanical pal and would soon become accustomed to its quaint staccato style. Even when improved techniques and increased computing power permit perfect intonation, it should be remembered that naturalness rather than perfection is the goal in the companion application. If and when we get to the desirable position of being able to achieve broadcast-level English generated by a machine, then we should artificially degrade it with the appropriate measure of hesitations, flaws, splutters, and mispronunciations that characterize everyday conversation. Despite present limitations, the impact of the speaking machine should not be underestimated. Experience suggests that even the mechincal voices of today convey far greater personality and "humanness" than could ever be achieved by any form of teletype output.

As the strangeness of the mechanical voice fades with familiarity and gradually ceases to provoke humor or irritation, we could well find that people's own speech patterns begin to change, developing the staccato style by "social contagion." And this might even help the machine to understand more readily the verbal output of the human speaker, for the comprehension of continuous speech is one of the most difficult tasks that the computer is expected to achieve.

Talking with Machines: We Talk to Them

It is easy to see why even recognition of single spoken words is difficult for a machine, for people speak with different accents, inflections, volumes, and speeds. The voice is as individual as one's fingerprint or handwriting, and even the same person's pronunciation of a word is likely to vary with mood, task, and social context. One speaker's "roast" may sound, in isolation, more like "roost," and to resolve the ambiguity human listeners home in on the correct interpretation by using a knowledge of the speaker's accent (we "correct" for known particularities in speech style) and by inferring from the context (we are unlikely to interpret our speaker as saying "roost beef"). Computers, too, can make corrections and allowances for the individual voice style and to some extent use context or sentence meaning to "disambiguate" words.

One of the first demonstrations of word recognition came nearly thirty years ago when a technologist constructed the "watermelon box." When anybody spoke the word "watermelon" into a microphone a red light came on. Since "watermelon" doesn't sound much like any other common word, not much discrimination was necessary for this task. Clearly, it would be more difficult to construct a device that responded only to "book," for example, because it could easily be confused with words such as "hook," "cook," and "bunk." Thus the number of words that can be adequately discriminated is a measure of the "power" of a speech-recognition system.

Machines that operate by voice control in industry today recognize spoken numbers and limited commands such as "cancel," "reorder," and "stock." Such machines are more accurate and more powerful when the program allows for a short training period in which the operator dictates a few times in his or her normal voice the full vocabulary with which the machine is to operate. This allows the machine to form an impression of the typical spectrogram produced by the speaker for each word and makes accuracy far greater during the operating period. It can be seen, also, how such a system would allow a machine to recognize familiar voices, so that the operator's "Hello" to the machine might bring the friendly response: "Hi, there, George. Where were you yesterday?"

Single-word speech-recognition systems have been incorporated into a number of children's toys and wheelchairs for the disabled (with commands such as "stop," "go," "turn left," and "slow"). They are also available to the home-computer enthusiast. The Apple II system, for example, currently has a 64-word speech-recognition package. This is not powerful compared to some of the more advanced systems, and IBM is now claiming that one of its developments has a total speech-recognition vocabulary of 1,500 words. While this represents only a fraction of the size of a reasonable dictionary (80,000 words), ordinary spoken speech contains some 10,000 words and "social chatting" employs even less. In "Basic English," which was invented by C. K. Ogden in the 1930s, the English language was reduced to only 850 words, and despite this apparently severe limitation complex books were written using only the permitted vocabulary and the appropriate conventions ("hive," for example, became "bee-house").

There is, however, a world of difference between being able to recognize 1,500 words spoken individually and being able to decipher them within the continuous sound spectrogram that characterizes normal speech. Words flow into one another, and the difference between, say, "car's top" and "car stop" must come from the context. Even single-word recognition faces a similar problem with homonyms such as "leak" and "leek." We cannot long escape the central problem, then, of the need to analyze "meaning." Even in research programs aimed only at machine transcription (typing) of dictated speech rather than at machine understanding, the analysis of meaning has been shown to be essential. While single-word recognition principally involves the mechanical process of analyzing sound spectrums and then matching the pattern to that of one of a limited set of words in a "dictionary," the process of analyzing continuous speech involves understanding and intelligence. Hard *technology* on its own cannot solve such problems, and we need software *techniques* to do the job. The development of software strategies for solving this and similar problems is one of the main tasks of artificial intelligence which we now need to consider before returning to the thorny problem of conversing with machines.

Artificial Intelligence

Artificial intelligence (known as AI—the context usually prevents any confusion with "artificial insemination") is concerned with producing programs that emulate certain human or animal functions, particularly those that we normally refer to as "intelligent," like complex problem solving. AI, then, is not about flashing lights and chips but about programs, which are themselves ways of handling given information. Intelligence in this context may be said to be about the step from the "given" to the "inferred." AI people often have a rather disdainful view of the computers themselves and treat them as mere "tools" for the realization of programs. The novelist may use a typewriter as an aid to writing, but it is merely an aid to realizing the product, it is not what novel writing is all about. Similarly, for AI workers it's the program that counts, not the hardware.

The field of artificial intelligence is a mixture of computer science, mathematics, psychology, linguistics, and philosophy. One of its aims, related principally to psychology, is to understand more about the real human processes of cognition and perception with the aid of computer programs. If we are able to simulate a process, then this gives us some idea of what *might* be going on "in nature." Most of the efforts of AI workers working within a psychological framework have been devoted to understanding basic processes of thinking and perception, but there is now increasing interest in the areas of social judgment and social interaction.

The relationship between symbols, words, and objects is the subject matter of linguistics, and many AI projects also explore this field, basing their analyses on the processes of "information use," which form a central part of the general computer-science field. The problems encountered in this and other AI enterprises, however, are not just technical but raise fundamental issues about the nature of knowledge, the nature of a person, and many areas of conceptual analysis that are more often discussed under the headings of the philosophy of knowledge and the philosophy of mind. Finally, another aim of AI, and one that gives it special research impetus, concerns the solving of those software problems that impede the construction of intelligent machines.

AI software is especially innovative and sophisticated, and consideration of work in the field soon exposes the falsehood of many popular myths concerning the nature of programs. One such myth is that programs carry out only what the programmer intended. This just isn't true. Programs may be self-adaptive, they may learn by experience, they can incorporate exploratory routines, and they may have several random functions, with the result that the programmer, having set the program on the machine, may be quite surprised by the output and may not even recognize it as having been produced by the program that he or she has written.

One question that has taxed the thinking of philosophers for some time is: "Can a machine be conscious?" This raises the obvious and difficult problem of what is meant by consciousness, and the initial question remains a highly controversial one, but some, at least, are convinced that a positive answer should be given. The argument is put forward that the machine can be made "aware" of its decisions and of the processes it is using and can "know" its governing goals, or "motives." It can monitor its own performance and "realize" where it is, what it is doing, and where it "intends" to go from there.

Obviously, the words "intend," "realize," "know," and "aware" are themselves all psychological terms, and we are not accustomed to extending their use to machines, but some people have argued that such arbitrary restriction is mere biological chauvinism. We might be happier saying that the computer-based system operates *as if* it were conscious. In terms of what the machine actually *does*, the behavior might be precisely the same whether it is conscious or isn't, and given this position we might feel that we can leave the philosophers to debate the question of whether a machine can or cannot be conscious. For our purposes, we can surely be content with the fact that there is apparently nothing in principle to stop a machine from behaving *as if it were conscious* in the way in which we believe humans to be conscious. It has been suggested that there might be limitations to the "insight" that machines might have of their hardware and the "nature of their being," but they're hardly alone in that. It can be argued that levels of existential awareness and knowledge of brain processes are also low for humans, so that they, too, can be said to have little insight into their hardware or true being.

Historically, AI grew out of cybernetics, variously defined as "the science of control" and "the science of effective organization." Early cybernetics explored the effects of feedback within a system and developed strategies for conducting searches in order to find solutions to problems. Cybernetic machines were invented that had the ability to seek and learn and to adjust to optimal conditions, depending on the quality of the environment. AI similarly involves procedures for searching out optimal strategies, goals, and solutions. The simplest type of search is a purely random one. If a target is known, then an exhaustive search will eventually reveal whether or not it is present in a field. But with structured material it is plainly better to have an organized search, and a method that directs such a quest along promising pathways is known as "heuristic." AI is largely about such systematic strategies for finding solutions to problems, and these problems might involve tasks like the identification of an object in the physical world, the understanding of a sentence, or the production of a well-structured and meaningful reply to a question.

The most advanced AI projects are concerned with situations in which the goal itself may not be too clear and in which solutions therefore need to be found to vague and ill-defined problems. AI programs may look for shortcuts and "make the best of a bad job" where other programs would be less flexible; they play on hunches and may use metaphors and analogies in their reasoning. Sometimes such programs come up with highly innovative and original solutions, and they also learn by experience. Through their "experience bank" they can develop a limited worldview extending their repertoire of problem-solving skills and enabling them to apply a strategy learned in one task to a quite different problem.

Understanding the Visual World

For two of the most exciting AI projects, those concerned with the perceptual analysis of the visual world and the analysis of verbal meaning, the notion of a machine's "picture of the world" has proved to be of enormous importance. A camera might be able to produce a representation of the physical world, but it can't be said to "see," since seeing is an active process that involves the recognition and differentiation of stimuli. Such recognition is based on interpretation, which is itself based on prior knowledge about the nature of the world. We are often able to identify an object only because of the context in which it is seen, and a whole lifetime of experience may be involved in the inferences we make. For this reason it is by no means a simple thing to get machines to see the world, and it has become increasingly apparent that we must find some way of supplying them with knowledge about the nature of things and the contexts in which they may be expected to appear. In addition, more basic information will have to be provided about how appearance is affected by distance, lighting, and orientation.

An early machine that attempted to achieve visual discrimination was produced by the physicist John Taylor. He invented a machine that sexed people's photographs. Pictures were placed beneath a lens that focused the pattern of light and shade onto an array of light-sensitive devices. In an initial training period, as well as having all the data from the array, the machine was informed whether the photograph was that of a man or a woman, but after a hundred or so training trials the machine had learned to correctly identify the sex of the portrait. Clearly, it was recognizing the sex from some pattern in the data from the array of photosensors, but quite what this pattern looked like was unknown even to the man who invented the machine. Perhaps we shouldn't be too surprised at this, for many human skills, like the sexing of faces, are performed reliably without the individual being able to formulate the implicit rules that must be followed for such a feat to be possible. The importance of this exercise for understanding machine potential is that it demonstrates that we don't necessarily have to provide a step-by-step breakdown of a process for a machine to be able to pick up a skill. Provided we give it adequate training, it may be able to solve the problem in its own enigmatic way.

There is now no problem with the hardware at the "front end" of a visual recognition system. A television camera can be automatically focused on a scene and the resulting picture readily "digitized" so that all the information in the picture is represented by a sequence of numbers or "0"s and "1"s. A normal television picture is made up of dots of light, shade, and dark (normally there are eight levels of brightness) arranged in 625 lines down the screen and with about 600 separate positions along each line. Each position or "picture cell" (pixcel) thus provides information that can be digitized. Because the television picture changes twenty-five times a second the information load is very large, though this can be considerably reduced by having fewer and larger pixels (thereby losing some of the definition of the picture) and by noting only the changes from frame to frame. There is, then, little problem in registering the picture input. The problem comes with trying to interpret that input.

There are many different AI programs for visual recognition, but certain themes are common to most of them. One strategy involves seeking out the edges first, as we do when starting a jigsaw puzzle. By looking for points of high light intensity contrast and then joining these together, there is some hope of being able to sort out the objects from the background. If the program makes the assumption that it inhabits a world of regular geometrical shapes (and most programs are geared precisely to such an environment), then the overlapping of objects can be compensated for by the program "guessing" that an edge that disappears behind an object and then emerges "on course" is in fact continuous. Making the appropriate allowances for shadows can be a tricky problem, but with complex geometry and intelligent guesswork this difficulty has been solved by a number of programs. It's easy to say that recognition also takes into account the context, but it must be realized that the context data are often as messy as that of the object we are trying to recognize, and AI work has shown us just how chaotic raw visual data can be.

A general approach that has proved very useful is that of taking certain clues from input, hypothesizing that these come from a particular object or shape, and then seeking further information to verify or refute the original hypothesis. Many psychologists argue that such a procedure underlies the process of human perception. Contemporary machine systems don't come anywhere near the sophistication of human vision, but certain of their achievements are undoubtedly impressive. There are now systems that interpret solid geometrical shapes from line drawings, that correctly identify solid objects (such as cubes, bricks, and rods) whatever their orientation or relative position, and that interpret a sequence of pictures in terms of the movement they portray. One program is designed to allow the machine to recognize people from photographs by matching the outline of the head to one of a range of familiar faces, another enables it to differentiate between over twenty archaeologically important types of Greek vases, and another produces identification of a Peanuts cartoon. The computer might recognize Snoopy and Charlie Brown, the kennel and the baseball bat, but that's about its limit, though we can at least conceive of a program that "understands" the cartoon.

For all of these accomplishments in the field of visual recognition, the program needs to know certain facts about the world. This illustrates a fact that psychologists have been emphasizing for a long time, that "there is more to visual perception than meets the eye." The formidable problems encountered by AI programs in the field suggest that we cannot expect high-level visual skills from domestic computer systems for many years to come. This would impose some constraints on the range of interaction that is possible, but we do, of course, have close and unimpaired relationships with friends who are totally blind. Clearly, the necessary conditions for a satisfactory social interaction don't include a companion's ability to see, although they do include the potential for some sort of interactive contact. So far, machines "see" only in a rudimentary fashion, and improvements in this field will come through programs that are complex and imaginative enough to provide an adequate understanding of the world. A shortcut to understanding is often provided by using verbal description, and in this field there are major program developments, the results of which are likely to lead to considerable advances in computer vision. Thus the severe visual handicap that any presently constructed companion machine would certainly have is likely to be only a temporary disability.

Understanding the Language World

The task of providing a machine with hearing is subject to many of the same problems as those involved in giving it sight. This is not the case with "single-word recognition"—which involves matching a sound pattern with one of a preset number of stored patterns—but it is true for the understanding of natural speech input. In this case we must help the machine to use contextual cues and a general knowledge of the world to recognize and understand what is going on. The microphone picks up all the available audio information, just as the camera is sensitive to visual input, but it cannot be said to "hear," for hearing is an active and constructive process and its efficiency depends greatly on our level of understanding.

The practical aims of speech-recognition projects cover a wide range. We would want a machine to operate on verbal commands, we would want it to produce written text directly from dictation, and we would, of course, want to hold natural conversations with it. Eventually the machine might provide us with instant translation from one natural tongue to another. The dream of such an "automatic translator" has long been with us, and such apparatus is standard equipment for characters in science fiction who converse with aliens. Initially we'd be very happy with a computer that rendered spoken Japanese or French into English, but before this happens we would expect a machine to be able to translate typed input. There is considerable overlap between speech recognition and the understanding of written text, and if we first examine the latter we can then consider the additional features of systems designed for the comprehension of continuous speech.

Before the advent of AI, attempts at the machine translation of written text involved a simple matching of key words and phrases together with a very simple grammatical analysis, but the results of these efforts were far from acceptable. The truth of the matter is that translation involves comprehension at a very high level, and AI programs attempt to improve matters by providing the machine with a store of background knowledge and allowing it to produce a meaning analysis of the context beyond that of the sentence currently under examination. The process actually involves a double translation, for the machine takes the initial sentence and then analyzes it and transforms it into an abstract pattern of symbols that would be quite meaningless to a human observer but that might be said to represent the "core meaning" of the sentence. Working from this it now produces a meaningful translation into the second natural language.

Formal text differs considerably from a transcription of natural speech, and to understand even typed "conversation" the computer needs to have some knowledge of human speech style. The conversational mode is less explicit, and a single word or phrase may be used to convey a great deal of information. This is because the speaker knows the person he or she is speaking to and because the individuals involved have a history of shared interaction. Recent verbal exchanges may have set the scene so that the restatement of information to give each sentence an independent meaning would result in a lot of verbal redundancy.

If you suddenly come in on the middle of a conversation, then the first sentences you hear are often impossible to understand. "Well, OK, I'll do it," says one. "But not unless he has," replies the other. *They* understand what they're talking about but *we* don't—we've missed out on the context that has already been set. If two people know each other extremely well, then whole chunks of their personalized jargon might be opaque to the casual listener. There are, of course, patterns and rules that describe conversational flow, and these are studied in "discourse analysis." Attempts at natural language programming, even where keyboard rather than speech input is involved, make it clear that to obtain full natural conversation between human and computer the machine will have to be provided with a good deal of insight into human discourse, human interaction styles and the rules which govern our social world. Only if there is sufficient overlap between the experiential worlds of the person and the machine will the two be able to converse and fully understand one another.

As with translation, the early attempts at keyboard conversation involved simple grammatical analysis and the identification of key words and phrases, automatic responses to these being produced according to a preset format. Of the many programs using such a strategy, the most famous is Joseph Weizenbaum's ELIZA, and this is designed to perform as a "nondirective therapist." The "client" sits before the keyboard typing in statements about feelings and relationships, and the computer responds in therapist fashion, asking for clarification, reflecting back the feelings which the client is disclosing, and probing more deeply into problems. ELIZA was conceived principally as a research exercise designed to show how conversation with a machine was possible. The therapy framework was used because the responses of a human therapist using this style of counseling conform to a systematic and stereotyped pattern. However, despite its limitations, many people seem to enjoy their sessions with ELIZA, and they often confide real problems. Some, indeed, claim that ELIZA's therapy has given them considerable psychological help. It is clear that many people soon forget that they are interacting with a machine and come to regard the system as they would a human therapist. When it was once suggested that conversations should be recorded by the machine to be read and studied later by research workers, the objection was raised that this would constitute a gross invasion of privacy.

The following conversation is part of a recent session I had with ELIZA:

ELIZA: Hi, I'm Eliza, what's your problem?
NEIL: I feel tired
ELIZA: Tell me more about such feelings
NEIL: I'm not alert
ELIZA: Did you come to me because you're not alert?
NEIL: Yes
ELIZA: Are you sure?

NEIL: Maybe I have other problems too
ELIZA: You don't seem quite certain
NEIL: Sorry
ELIZA: Please don't apologize

This may look impressive and "intelligent," but it is really a pseudoconversation. The machine has been programmed to recognize certain words and letter sequences and then respond to these in a prearranged way. For example, it scans for the letters "hi" and "who" and treats these respectively as a greeting and a question even when they form part of longer words, as in the following example from a less successful meeting I had with ELIZA:

NEIL: I have a whole lot of problems
ELIZA: Why do you ask?
NEIL: I don't want to hide anything
ELIZA: How do you do?

The disaster resulting from another of our interactions stems from more fundamental problems with ELIZA's lack of understanding:

ELIZA: Do you often feel sad?
NEIL: No
ELIZA: Are you saying no just to be negative?
NEIL: Not at all
ELIZA: Please don't repeat yourself
NEIL: I'm not
ELIZA: Did you come to me because you are not?
NEIL: Not what?
ELIZA: Why do you ask?
NEIL: Now I'm really confused
ELIZA: How long have you been really confused?
NEIL: Only since I met you

Clearly, ELIZA has considerable limitations, and many of these are in fact fundamental to the overall strategy used in the type of program that attempts to use language without understanding it. ELIZA is cleverly contrived to "converse," but no attempt is made to get her to comprehend the statements being made and so we should not be too surprised when she makes a howler. Similar blunders frequently appear in text translation programs that rely on word equivalence and that attempt to function without an analysis of meaning. Margaret Boden, a leading writer in the field of AI, has provided several examples of the type of mistake that a word-swap translation program might produce, including "The spirit is willing, but the flesh is weak" rendered as "The whisky is fine, but the steak is not so good."

A keyboard-based conversational system that does introduce understanding and knowledge of the world into the dialogue is Terry Winograd's SHRDLU. This inhabits a limited conversational world in which the talk is about blocks of different shapes, sizes, and colors, and the vocabulary is restricted to about 200 words. The system "knows" the properties of these blocks and can be given instructions for moving them about. If told to place one block on top of another, for example, it can tell you whether or not this is possible (thus it knows that a cube won't easily balance on top of a pyramid). When you ask it questions about its world in natural conversational style, it can tell you, for instance, which shape is behind the yellow pyramid, how many things are shorter than the blue block, and how many objects there are inside a box.

If there are two green blocks and you instruct it to place "the green block" in the box, then it will quite properly demand: "Which green block?" If two successive instructions are: "Move the red pyramid to the left" and "Now move it to the right," the program will understand what "it" refers to in the second sentence, so that the analysis takes into account features of the whole conversation in deciding the meaning of any one sentence. Winograd's program is a milestone and demonstrates how well a computer can deal with language when it can understand what is being said. Conversations about blocks may not be intrinsically very exciting, but the achievement is important because it represents the fundamental leap from a machine merely *responding* to language to really *understanding* it. Following SHRDLU a number of other comprehension programs have been written by AI workers. Eugene Charniak has outlined one for understanding simple children's stories that incorporates a primitive model of human motives and intentions, and John Seely-Brown has created the interactive system SOPHIE to teach students of electronics how to search for faults in electrical circuits.

Each of these programs has a very specific verbal environment, or "universe of discourse," and is completely ignorant of the world beyond it. SHRDLU and SOPHIE would be completely useless for analyzing children's fiction, and Charniak's story program would be dumfounded if we told it about transistors and resistors. At any one time a conversation between two people is also likely to be focused within a rather limited verbal arena, but people are very flexible in switching from one topic to another and are highly skilled at recognizing the cues for such a change. Marvin Minsky has introduced the concept of a "frame," which is a chunk of knowledge relating to a particular type of context such as a children's party or an office situation. The idea is that a machine might operate with many alternative frames, such as "physical blocks," "social introduction," "the neighbors," and "the weather," and might then switch from one to another as appropriate. A computer could clarify which type of situation it is in by identifying key concepts and using these as cues for change. It might also take the initiative in changing frames during informal social interaction and thus play a full part in shaping the verbal context. On the basis of its experience in different situations, the computer would also be able to create whole new frames for itself, initiating rather than simply responding to topics of conversation.

The work on the understanding of printed sentences forms a basis on which much of the recent work on continuous speech-recognition systems depends. As we have seen, machine recognition of single words is not now a problem, but to enable a computer to make sense of a naturally spoken sentence we need to build in meaning analysis strategies. The system is then in a position to make accurate guesses as to how the sound flow can be broken down into single-word units and to recognize what those words are. Homonyms such as "right" and "write" can in this way be correctly identified. The relationship between the meaning of a sentence and the interpretation of the sound pattern is a complex one, for not only does the meaning aid the unscrambling of the sound pattern, but the intonation also provides added cues to meaning. Thus the intonation of a spoken sentence often makes the intention clearer than would the written form, and "disambiguates" it.

In the United States, Donald Walker is developing a system capable of understanding and analyzing the sounds of sentences spoken by a human operator. The complex program first examines the likely grammatical structure of the statement, and the acoustics are then converted into digital form and sorted into various classes of sound, such as "vowels" and "silence." The machine's understanding of the words is now verified, the program checking whether initial analyses of words make sense in the context of the whole sentence. The now-familiar strategy of first hypothesizing and then testing is therefore once again in operation. Any contextual help in homing in on the correct hypothesis is obviously a great advantage. When a program called HEARSAY plays "voice chess," it uses a knowledge of the rules of the game and the present state of the board to predict what the opponent is likely to say next and then uses this to interpret the speech input.

The transcription of spoken material by a "typewriter

with ears" has obvious and immediate commercial application, and the race is therefore on to produce the first machine of this type. Toshiba currently appears to be in the lead and has promised that such a system will be available within the next few years. The flexibility of current word processors is such that when they are linked to a transcription device, office correspondence will be efficiently produced even if there are initial transcription errors, for such mistakes can be rectified by the operator's repeating, or if necessary spelling out, the incorrect words.

Synthetic speech output can also benefit from an AI-based analysis of meaning. At present, such output lacks naturalness because of its rather bland intonation, but current studies of the relationship between meaning and intonation will provide a theoretical basis for a program linking a speech synthesizer with a "meaning analysis program" so that the sounds of natural speech may be produced. Scientists at Bell Laboratories have created a program that simulates the human mouth and vocal cords. The machine has a large word-sound dictionary and a knowledge of grammar. By following complex rules of intonation, it produces sentences that have some degree of naturalness in terms of stress, pitch, and timing.

Natural intonation reflects the grammatical structure of the sentence and its meaning, but it is also affected by the personal style of the speaker and his or her intentions and feelings at that time. All actors realize that the right intonation depends not only on understanding the text but also on knowing the full dramatic context and being "in role." A skilled performer may be able to speak the same sentence in numerous different ways both by making basic transformations in emphasis and timing, and by "feeling" it in different ways. Thus the development of adequate meaning analysis by machine will achieve only part of what it takes to speak naturally. A further step might have to be taken of programming into the system the equivalent of "feelings," so that a computer analyzing an insult input would respond with a hurt or angry intonation. An alternative strategy would be to train the computer in such skills by exposing it to a wide spectrum of the patterns of human intonation in different situations. The vocal repertoire of a system may, of course, be as wide as that of a human being. Machines will whisper secrets, laugh at puns, and cry at bad news. To say that someone "really understands me" is equivalent to saying that we feel close to that person. Some emotional involvement is frequently elicited even by such pseudoconversational programs as ELIZA, but this suggests that there is a much greater potential for intimacy in true meaning-analysis systems, and particularly if those systems can speak and hear. Natural language input and output would clearly go a long way toward increasing the approachability of machines, and it would reduce or eradicate the need for users to possess any technical knowledge about how to operate them. When computers were first introduced they had to be programmed directly in binary code. Programming languages made this unnecessary, and these were then used to enable an unskilled user to control the machine by typing ordinary English words such as "ADD" and "FILE." The latest developments mean that spoken commands (such as: "I wonder what the capital of Chile is," and "Could you tell me the square root of 1.985, please?") will be answered swiftly, accurately, pleasantly, and with appropriate intonation, and normal social conversation will also be possible. No other development will help as much in making computers the convivial companions that they can and will become.

Moving in the World: Robotics

So far our vision of the intelligent machine has been that of a rather sedentary computer sitting on a table-top. Ideally, however, we would want such machines to be able to perform useful tasks that involve movement, or we might just want one to follow us around under its own steam. The term "robot" usually conjures up a vision of a machine vaguely resembling a human in its appearance and functioning, but the robots now used in industry for manufacturing and assembling complex apparatus don't generally have a humanoid shape. They are strictly functional, and their complex movements are often not those that a person could or would make. The intense development of such machines may have led to great advances in movement engineering and control, but despite this, and although the achievements of walking dolls and clockwork automata have now been far surpassed, there is still no machine that can walk in the same way and with the same speed as that of a man or woman.

Because of the formidable problems, many of the projects in robotics have aimed instead at reproducing alternative forms of locomotion. Several of these employ wheeled systems, but designers have cast a wide scan over the biological world and ideas have been borrowed from insect movement, crab walking, and turtle trotting. The Japanese workers Hirose and Umetani studied the natural motion of snakes and then built the Active Cord Mechanism, a thin, long robot that wriggles its way across surfaces. Innovative it may be, but probably not a thing we'd want sliding about the house.

Biological systems have also been a source of inspiration for robotologists in several other ways. One branch of biology, that which is based on the observation of animal behavior in natural settings, is known as ethology. A leading ethologist, Niko Tinbergen, has made an analysis of the relative status of different motives and instincts. He suggests that they form a hierarchical structure in terms of which takes precedence in controlling the animal's behavior at any one time, and this has been used by J. S. Albus in formulating a model of robot control.

Ethological studies of instinctive behavior in animals have also given rise to a number of other robot applications, and they continue the general strategy of imitating nature, which has a long and honored history in engineering and technology. Several computer developments have been stimulated by what is known about information processing in the human brain, but such borrowing can also be a two-way process, and many analyses of brain processes follow computer models.

Thirty years ago the British physiologist William Grey Walter built a wheeled "tortoise" that explored the environment. He endowed it with the mock biological name of *Machina speculatrix*. Running around the floor, it was attracted by lights, though if a light were too bright it would back away. This creation pushed small objects to the side and could find its way around heavy ones by nosing to and fro until it found its escape. It also avoided slopes which were too steep. The robot's little head was fitted with a light of its own and thus it would approach mirror reflections of itself and two such creatures of course found each other mutually attractive. When the batteries were running low, the "tortoise" would find its "hutch" and recharge them, "feeding" from the electrical power source.

Although the device consisted of only a handful of simple valves, relays, motors and the like it behaved in an amazingly life-like way and the inventor thus achieved his aim of showing that simple mechanisms can produce complex structured behavioral patterns. Furthermore, although some of the behavior was quite predictable some of it was quite unforeseen by Grey Walter and he couldn't always say exactly what was happening inside *Machina speculatrix*.

In the early 1960s some scientists at Johns Hopkins University built the Hopkins Beast, described as "a trashcan on wheels." The Beast could navigate its way through corridors using the sonar reflection method we commonly associate with bats. If it located a power socket, then it would carefully plug itself in for a shot of electricity. Several close cousins of the tortoise and the Beast were produced (including Edmund Berkeley's Squee, a "squirrel" that collected golf balls) before a walking machine was attempted. One of the first of these was produced at the Stanford Research Institute in California in 1970 and was remotely controlled by computer. It wasn't, however, very steady on its mechanical legs, and hence its name—Shakey!

Today a number of research teams in Japan, the Soviet Union, the United States, and Great Britain are working on projects aimed at the production of a computer-based walking biped. Such efforts have made it clear that walking locomotion is very complex indeed, involving computations that include such factors as gravity pull and the machine's own weight, position, and momentum. Advanced systems incorporate television cameras that survey the scene and require that the robot must be acutely familiar with its own body image and properties. Several machines can now walk in a straight line and stairs can be climbed effectively, but there are great difficulties involved in their walking over rough ground, turning round, and negotiating obstacles. Even when such navigation is successfully achieved, the process involves a great deal of computation and the movements are very slow.

Many industrial robots have arms that are similar to those of humans, but they often terminate in "pincers" rather than fingers. They may have sensors with which to feel the weight and texture of an object, but they have limited touch sensitivity. For some applications, it is easier to base the control of complex movements directly on human actions rather than by programming them artificially. One example of such copying of skilled movements is found in the process of spray-painting mass-manufactured items. A highly skilled human sprayer first has mechanical motion sensors strapped to his arms while he performs the standard spray job, and his movements are then recorded on magnetic tape. When the tape is replayed through the system, now minus the man, the paint is sprayed in a pattern precisely imitating the man's movements. The tape can be played again and again, copied and adjusted, and the automated spraying can continue twenty-four hours a day for 365 days a year without coffee breaks, holidays, sick leaves, or strikes. The man, of course, is without a job, but that's another story.

These developments mean that companion machines needn't be sedentary, but neither should we expect them, at least initially, to stroll beside us on a summer's walk. Most of our social interaction, in fact, takes place within a relatively small space, and much of it is conducted with one or both people sitting and moving little. This doesn't at all interfere with the social process, and, of course, we relate perfectly well to people who are chronically bedridden or confined to wheelchairs. Adventurous locomotion, then, should not be seen as a necessary feature of the companion machine, and what it lacks in this respect it may well make up for with its friendliness, civility, good humor, and intelligence. But one thing at least seems clearly indicated for the future story of technological accomplishment: a world-class chess machine will appear sometime before a world-class robot disco-dancer!

The Micro Supermarket

One feature of the new technology that has a special bearing on the viability of the companion micro is the amazing cheapness of it all. Despite the leap in complexity and sophistication (and in some ways because of this), the cost of the computers and computing has plummeted. It is estimated that in twenty years there has been an *annual* 30 percent drop in the cost of the vital processing components, so that the equivalent computing power now costs one-thousandth of what it did in the early 1960s. Certain items, like the casing and packaging, have not dropped substantially in price, and so the overall cost of a machine to the consumer might not have been reduced quite as dramatically as this figure suggests. Nevertheless, Victor Vyssotsky, an expert on the implementation of computers in business systems, has suggested that in the next twenty years the cost-performance ratio of processors and main memories will again improve by a factor of a hundred, and this view seems to reflect a general optimism within the industry.

Because research and development costs are very high and ongoing production costs so low, it is in the interest of producers to stimulate demand and to sell chip-based products in whatever form possible. Copies of microprocessors can be made by the million and the hundred million, and producers are therefore stumbling over each other to be innovative in the field of the mass market. Competition is ferocious, and the industry abounds with pirates who buy new chips fresh off the production line and then grind them down, taking high-power photographs at each stage so that they can copy them. This process is known as "reverse engineering." The basic architecture of the chip is not well protected by copyright laws, and many of those for sale on the open market are frankly described as based on another manufacturer's design.

Although many ready-made software companies have concentrated on the games market, an increasing number of manufacturers are imaginatively exploiting the more traditional computer functions associated with business and mathematics. But the home computer's major asset is its flexibility, and with add-on units it can be made to perform a vast spectrum of tasks. Speech recognition and generation is available for a number of models, and some can be transformed into music synthesizers, "painting" apparatus (in which the computer controls the colors appearing on a TV screen), and poetry writing machines. Some can understand handwritten input and learn to recognize the handwriting of a particular person. Conversational packages such as ELIZA are also on sale. So far, the people who have been buying these machines have generally been hobbyists who have some interest in programming itself, but there is now a new generation of machines that are more easily operated and in which simple commands or plug-in cartridges are sufficient to change the machine from one task to another. Texas Instruments, for example, is marketing its model 99/4, which speaks to the user and will play games, plan diets, and suggest menus.

In 1981 Commodore introduced a low-priced machine called VIC, a color computer with sound and high-resolution graphics. A range of plug-in cartridges gives the machine wide appeal and allows users to progress from ready-made games to sophisticated programs of their own. IBM also launched its own up-market personal computer. In 1982 Acorn, in Britain, cooperated with the BBC to produce a machine linked to a series of television programs aimed at making a wider public computer conscious. In the same year Clive Sinclair, renowned for his ultra-low-cost ZX80 and ZX81 models (the latter of which later appeared in the U.S. as the Timex/Sinclair 1000), introduced his most remarkable product to date, Spectrum. In 1983 Apple launched LISA, a machine with a remarkably high degree of user friendliness.

The low cost and wide availability of such items has been matched by a consumer interest that seems insatiable. Monthly computer magazines, with listings of programs ready to be typed into the popular models, started to multiply, all aimed at the amateur enthusiast who owns, or is about to own, a home computer. At the same time, schools received government encouragement to get at least one machine in every secondary school as soon as possible. There are also a number of computer summer camps in which children and families learn to program, play games, and operate miniature robot systems.

All these developments add up to a movement in which millions of nontechnical people will soon get direct, hands-on experience of computers. Once they gain some proficiency at the skills involved, they will be looking for new games and projects on which to exercise their expertise. Many will use the opportunity to explore the imaginative and creative potential of computers, and some will develop their own solutions to the problem of simulating human and social elements.

Besides the all-purpose home computer there are smaller units that are dedicated solely to one particular function. There are machines that play bridge (coping with three hands simultaneously for the lone bridge player) and others which give a good game of chess, checkers, and backgammon. There is now a backgammon program that can beat all comers, including the (human) world champion, although this is not yet available in a commercial unit. Domestic chess-playing machines can beat a good amateur player, but they generally have a skill-control feature that can be used to set the sophistication of play so that the beginner is not trounced in a moment. Chess-playing machines can also replay world-chess games, teach chess to beginners, and recall the complete sequence of moves in a game just played. There is one version that speaks its moves and then congratulates or commiserates with the human opponent at the end of the game.

Some of the children's toys and educational devices that use the new technology indicate the manufacturers' intention to design appealing apparatus for maximum sales penetration of the domestic market. "George" is a voice-operated delivery van that, in response to verbal commands, moves forward or backward, turns left or right, and stops and starts. The same technology has been employed in voice-controlled wheelchairs, and this provides an excellent example of how technology can be used to help the disabled. Another example is the machine that speaks aloud from printed text, which it reads through its television eye, and that may well revolutionize the world of the blind. It's more difficult to think of a serious social benefit to be derived from the technology involved in "Ben," the toy dog that walks, barks, and wags his tail in response to whistles and claps.

The educational toy "Speak and Spell," which is manufactured by Texas Instruments, is aimed at teaching children to spell. After hearing the machine speak a target word, the child keys in the supposed spelling and is then told if he or she is correct. If there are a few successive failures the machine spells the word aloud and displays the correct spelling. The original voice synthesizer employed in "Speak and Spell" had a pronounced American accent, but the latest model employs a British voice for the British market. The machine is small and colorful and, remarkably, sells for less than sixty dollars. It exemplifies the new low cost and wide availability of very sophisticated circuitry.

The race to sell chips has produced some devices that are highly functional necessities but also, incidentally, some gadgetry that appears exorbitant in its use of high technology. Toshiba, for example, has produced voice-operated television and hi-fi, and the Windart Watch Company manufactures a watch that speaks the time—in four languages. There is also a Japanese vending machine that, when it senses the presence of a human, says "Welcome" and after use thanks the purchaser and reminds him not to forget the change. There are also many "composites," some of which, including the combination "calculator–alarm clock–dictating machine–radio–cigarette lighter," appear to have been designed by someone drunk with the power of miniaturization. Television sets with a two-inch screen seem to be another example of the philosophy that says: "It *can* be done, so let's do it." The aim, of course, is to sell, to infiltrate markets, to expand markets, and to create markets. And the competition is so fierce that almost any avenue, including the bizarre, is likely to be explored.

It is for this reason that we should have no doubt that the manufacture of companion machines will very soon be an area of intense marketing activity. In this chapter I have indicated the technological feasibility of a machine that would act as a companion. The individual elements are there, albeit in separate packages, and with suitable software and a suitable "shell" the companion micro will certainly emerge. Economic feasibility also seems assured. Costs are falling all the time, and aggressive manufacturers are looking for any market that stands half a chance of bringing financial reward. And we are, of course, talking of a market that is potentially worth many millions of dollars.

There are already the first stirrings of interest in such a project. Several companies are designing domestic robots, with some primitive machines already being offered for sale; the domestic computer is already fully on the market. The target functions for such machines concern household chores, information, and games rather than friendly interaction, but this is soon likely to change.

The technology explosion that derived from the needs of industry, business, and the military has incidentally given us the means to facilitate and explore a new type of social interaction. But will people accept such changes? Will they let themselves be seduced into "social" relationships with chips? Surely there is a "machine barrier" that will inhibit such free intercourse between people and machines?

PART TWO

ENCOUN-
TERING THE
INANIMATE

CHAPTER 3

Personal Involvement with Computers

Emotional Responses to the Computer

One popular image of the computer is that of a cold, metallic object with flashing lights and spinning magnetic tapes, the very essence of the physical, impersonal machine. This image portrays the computer as an advanced calculator, cool, objective, and unapproachable. Yet quite different images are possible, and emotional reactions to such machines may be very strong. It is possible to hate them and to love them. The negative feelings may strike a more familiar chord. We are used to stories about computers that send out electricity bills sternly demanding the sum of $00.00 or a million dollars, of muddled holidays and ridiculous orders for a thousand pairs of socks. Few of these travesties are actually the result of machine failure, and most can be traced back to programming or operator error—that is, to humans. The machine is often a handy scapegoat, however, and may be held to blame for "bugs," or mistakes in which it has played no part.

However, it is obvious that computers *can* be very irritating. Experienced operators interacting with a faulty system or program can be overwhelmed by a particularly debilitating form of frustration. Tracing an error may take a very long time, and a bug can produce anxiety, despair, or anger. More than one computer installation has been wrecked by a systems operator who went berserk, damaging terminals, attacking the machine itself, and destroying priceless data. The disastrous consequences of such outbursts have now provoked computer companies to finance psychological research aimed at eliminating those systems features that elicit such resentment and violence. The outcome of these studies will be the development of programs and hardware that are more soothing and benevolent and that optimize that highly desirable quality, "user-friendliness."

Until now the design of computer systems has been highly functional. There has been a good deal of research into the characteristics of displays and teletypes in order to decrease the frequency of operator errors, but little attention has been paid to the machine's overall approachability. Consequently, the first appearance of the computer may be rather daunting, and the uninitiated may have to be coaxed into their first interaction. A little experience changes this, however, and an affection for the machine can soon develop. The computer may also become heavily personalized. This occurs in some purely working relationships (even "number crunchers" are often given names and said to "have moods"), but the effect is greatly enhanced when a more personal interaction takes place.

One form of such social interaction occurs when a sense of competition grows between the person and the computer. Even casual observation suggests that the player is frequently emotionally stirred by the electronic opponent and may project a personality onto the machine. Two American social psychologists, Karl Scheibe and Margaret Erwin, studied this tendency to treat the game-playing machine as if it were a person. They arranged for their students to play a series of games on a computer and they left a tape-recorder running while the action took place. The spontaneous comments indicated that all but one of their forty subjects personified the machine.

Scheibe and Erwin found that pronoun references were very common. The machine was referred to as "it," "he," "you," and "they," but, perhaps significantly, never as "she." One subject used the name "Fred," while others referred to it as "that guy." There were a number of comments about the computer that revealed a personification. These included: "It's just waiting for me to do it," "It's trying to con us," and "It's got a little mind." The experimenters also reported that "the use of profanity was common." It is interesting that interaction with computers frequently produces strong language and that many of the comments addressed to the machine via the terminal are obscene. At one American university the computer is preprogrammed to recognize certain taboo words, and if one of these is used it stops processing and demands an apology. If no apology is forthcoming the machine promptly switches off.

A research fellow in computing at the Royal College of Art in London has written a number of programs designed to deal with people who swear at or insult the machine. A program called ABUSE gets more and more nasty as the insult match escalates, while another routinely responds to any short sentence ending in "off" with "And you, too!" A machine will not always have the last word, however, and can be tricked into using obscenities itself. The story is told of a group of teenage boys who visited a science exhibition in which a computer demonstrated an "Animal Guessing Game." To play this the person had to think of an animal and the machine would then ask a series of questions, such as: "Is it warm-blooded?" until it was able to pinpoint the correct species.

If the machine was unable to identify the animal after a fixed number of questions, it would admit defeat and then ask the person to type in a question that would have enabled it to guess correctly. This was then stored, to be used if any similar situation occurred in the future. The boys had chosen as their animal "a girl," and the unsuccessful machine has been provided with a "vital question" that was obscene. Nevertheless, it remains in the computer memory, and when unsuspecting members of the public think of a particularly exotic animal they are likely to be asked: "Would you like to screw it?"

The animistic effect is greatly increased if the machine is able to speak. The voice synthesizer incorporated in Texas Instruments' "Speak and Spell" is rather hard and schoolmasterly, but, despite this, children relate to the instrument in a personal way. Adrian Hope, a writer in the field of electronics, discovered a way in which the animistic features of "Speak and Spell" could be enhanced. An extra memory (or ROM) can be added to the basic apparatus in the form of a small plug-in module, and for this to be used a button on the main instrument must be pressed. "If you press the 'module' key, but fail to insert the module," writes Hope, "the synthesizer circuitry makes its usual random search for instructions and will sooner or later delve into the nonexistent ROM. When this happens the synthesizer goes haywire, asking the operator to spell nonexistent words, phrases and sounds. So pathetic is the garbled sound that only the hardest heart could fail to feel sorry for the confused electronics, burbling as if in its final demented death throes."

Another key stimulus to animistic thinking is the presence of apparent intelligence. This is most clearly found in a computer that has been programmed to play chess, and players often report that they feel as if the machine is another person working out the best strategy and anticipating their own thinking. David Levy, the chess master, described how in his contest with one of the best available programs it was difficult for him to believe that he was not playing with a human opponent. The animistic tendency is brought to bear on many kinds of physical objects, but the computer is particularly powerful at elicting this type of thinking because it can respond interactively, flexibly, and verbally. Humor, surprise, and insult can all be written into a program, and the responses of the machine can be modeled on those of people. This aspect of programming has not been fully exploited so far, but there can be no doubt that the flexibility of the machine provides astonishing opportunities for such development.

Most people have little opportunity to interact personally with a friendly and intelligent machine. Like the surgical operating theater and the mortician's parlor, the computer installation may appear to be an unwholesome environment best left in the hands of the initiated. The barrage of specialized jargon and the image of unfathomable machines have done much to produce an unfortunate division between the experts on the one hand and the public on the other. A growing awareness of this lamentable dichotomy has led to several recent attempts to bridge the gap. Some of these have taken the form of popular books to demystify the machine by arranging personal introductions and others have involved, literally, taking the machine out onto the streets. In the project "Computertown USA!" Bob Albrecht and Roman Zamora have been taking their microcomputers into local bookshops and pizza parlors and inviting anyone who is interested to interact with the machines. They aim to bring computer awareness to the community at a grassroots level. Their efforts are largely aimed at children, and the hundreds of kids who have been involved have each been given a badge that reads: "My computer likes me." Teaching by adults is kept to a minimum—the computer is itself very helpful and the children help each other. There is even a "Rent-a-Kid" scheme in which children initiate adults into the magic of the machine. A similar scheme—"Computertown UK!"—has now been started in Britain, and once again children are the prime targets. David Tebbutt and Peter Rodwell, who introduced the project, write: "Children represent the weak point in society's anti-technology mental block and CTUK! is designed to take advantage of this." Their campaign slogan, aimed at the computer hobbyists who are encouraged to take their home-based machines out into the streets and cafés, is: "Bring Computer Literacy to Your Town."

The impact of the Computertown projects will be greatly amplified by hardware and software manufacturers seeking to create new markets. Powerful advertising, hard promotion, and systems with optimal approachability will certainly lead to the breakdown of the reserve that people now have about computers. We have already seen the exploitation of potential markets in the case of chip-based calculators, which are useful, and chip-based TV games, which are fun. Function and fun are the vital elements that will send chips flooding across the sales counter. To increase the market further, machines that are even more useful than calculators and even more fun than the current TV games will have to be produced. The present image of the computer as an advanced calculator can and will be changed, so that, in time, the machine will come to be seen as a potential companion, fully capable of taking part in a significant social interaction with the user.

There is every indication that the effects of this metamorphosis will be very powerful. Installations with large computers may be enigmatic to most of us, but they are, of course, occupied by colonies of enthusiasts. When we look at the effects that computers have on some of *them*, we see an advance picture of what could happen to more ordinary mortals. Even though such machines are not "humanized," and even though the operators know a good deal about how the machines really work, the emotional impact of these computers can be considerable. For a foretaste of the likely effect on the near-future public, then, we should inspect the emotional world of the computer-initiated—the hackers!

Hacking with the Hackers

About fifteen years ago the computer scientist Joseph Weizenbaum announced that he had discovered a new personality type—the compulsive programmer. "People get hooked," he wrote; "they begin to behave in a way that resembles addiction. They refuse food, they refuse their girl-friends." In their paper "The Psychology of Robots," Henry Block and Herbert Ginsburg speak of " 'computerniks'—those starry-eyed young men who can be found loitering at computer installations at all hours of the day and night." But the term that has caught on most widely to describe such zealots is "hacker," and what they do, constantly, is known as "hacking."

The characteristics of hackers have now been described a number of times. They are fascinated by, addicted to, and even in love with the thinking machine. They are fanatical, singleminded, and devoted. They spend hours and hours coaxing the computer to perform extravagant tasks. They can hardly bear to be out of physical contact with the machine, and when they are they carry their printouts around with them. They prefer to associate with the machine rather than with human beings, although they may make exceptions for fellow hackers. The conversation then revolves around computers, programs, and programming. Hackers may speak to one another using a strange vocabulary. A "gweep" is a hacker suffering from overwork and a "glork" is a mild surprise. A "vanilla" program is plain and ordinary, definitely not brilliant or "cuspy." The uninitiated ("bletchers") would be able to determine the nature of the insults that a hacker hurls at them by reference to *The Hacker's Dictionary*, compiled by gweeps at several U.S. universities, save for one cuspy hacker strategy—the dictionary is not a printed book but a computer file.

There are both advantages and disadvantages to hacking. First of all, the hacker generally becomes a very proficient programmer, developing particular computer skills through constant practice and problem-solving. The analogy has been drawn more than once between the hacker and the dedicated musician. Secondly, the hacker makes a friend of the computer. There is constant companionship, and eventually, when the program is finally debugged, the machine really seems to "understand." Thirdly, the hackers are preoccupied, they have a vocation, a mission, a hobby that can take on the proportions of a religious quest. And the quest can be without end, for there are always additional programs that can be written, programs that are more elaborate, more powerful, and more refined. The hacker is not content with a program that merely works; it has to be written in a style that is elegant, to perform its task gracefully. The hacker has a purpose in his well-structured life, and constantly expanding horizons. There are the good days when things work out well and the whole world seems sunny, and the bad days when a depressing bug refuses to give up its secrets. Hackers talking about their preoccupation may have glazed eyes; they can see the true light at the end of their programming tunnel. For some, there can be no doubt, operating the system can have a deep existential relevance.

Then there are the negative effects, and it is these that have been stressed in the warnings of computer scientists and university doctors, and in the various confessions of ex-hackers. Joseph Weizenbaum paints a suitably lurid picture of the victims of this computing monomania:

. . . bright young men of dishevelled appearance, often with sunken glowing eyes . . . their arms tensed and waiting to fire their fingers, already poised to strike, at the buttons and keys on which their attention seems to be riveted as a gambler's on the rolling dice. When not so transfixed, they often sit at tables, strewn with computer outputs over which they pore like possessed students of a cabbalistic text. They work until they drop, twenty, thirty hours at a time. Their food, if they arrange it, is brought to them: coffee, Cokes, sandwiches. If possible they sleep in cots near the computer.

The first stage in the demise of the hacker is marked by a lack of interest in other subjects. Programming might have started out as an ancillary task in a student's special subject of physics, chemistry, or psychology, but it soon takes over as the dominating interest. Computing becomes an end in itself as the fledgling hacker gets sucked into the loop between the human and the computer. The "A" grade in computing which may result from the obsession is regarded as more than adequate compensation for the dismal "C's" in all other subjects. I have seen students who were initially persuaded, rather against their will, to use a computer for solving some statistical problem in psychology become addicted within a very short time. They lose all interest in the initial problem and prefer, instead, to concentrate on further abstract programming. Some university departments are so aware of the possibility of the compulsion taking over that they make efforts to prevent their brightest students from drowning in a sea of output.

The second stage in the hacker's social downfall involves a disturbance of normal habits. Meals are eaten irregularly, sleep cycles are disturbed, and leisure activities are pushed aside to allow time for more interaction with the machine. It is not difficult to get carried away with programming, and even the casual programmer can easily lose track of time. The intense involvement that can soon develop makes programming one of those rather rare activities in which time can cease to exist and the passage of hours goes by unnoticed. Psychologists have called this phenomenon "flow" and have studied some of

the conditions under which it occurs. There is no doubt
that flow is pleasurable. Hackers recognize it and enjoy
it. And it helps to disrupt their lives.

The third stage of hackerhood is characterized by profound social withdrawal. Several writers have suggested
that those people who most readily succumb are often
rather introverted and socially inept individuals even before the compulsion takes over. The computer acts as a
substitute for human friends, perhaps, but the infatuation
may also bring about the end of existing relationships.
In the final stages the hacker's personality undergoes a
fundamental change. He (or she, although hacking does
seem to be a sex-related disorder) becomes desocialized
through lack of human contact. The world is now seen
through a system of concepts in which feedback loops
and Fast Fouriers have taken over from friendship and
fun.

We can easily imagine the effects of hacking on family
life. A number of hackers' wives have now joined other
grass widows parted from their husbands by golf or
similar obsessional activities. In an article entitled "The
Men Who Fall for Their Computers," Jane McLoughlin
examined this new phenomenon. One hacker's wife re-
marked: "The whole thing started when he began to
work late at the office, and I began to think that there
was another woman. When he came home he was distant and vague, and preoccupied, and in the end I
accused him of having a mistress." Under such pressure
the hacker broke down and confessed: ". . . he began to
talk of the pleasure he got out of playing the weirdest
experimental games with the computer. . . . I couldn't
compete, not with a machine, for God's sake." This wife
stood by her afflicted husband and even expressed fears
about what might happen if the firm were to remove
him from his electronic friend: "I know it sounds funny,
but I'm afraid that losing that computer may break his
heart." Jane McLoughlin also met an ex-hacker who,

since his self-cure, had been able to look back with some pleasure at his early hacking days: "I'd kick that machine of mine into life, sing a snatch of 'Yes, sir, that's my baby' to get her going, and she did whatever I wanted."

Hackers not only are obsessed with the programming but also often have a deep affection for the machine itself. They explore one side of their personality and develop one aspect of their skills with a singlemindedness that has obvious disadvantages. Some regard what they do simply as a form of legitimate adult play, while others take it far more seriously and see themselves as going beyond present human limitations, journeying into a new galaxy of knowledge in a way which they find at least as exciting as the exploration of deep space. However, the dismal picture that some computer scientists have painted of hackerhood, it should be noted, applies only to extreme cases. Any powerfully gripping activity will produce its casualties, and many programmers find their relationship with the machine exciting and satisfying without being completely taken over by it. They are the social drinkers in the picture, while the hackers are the alcoholics. The existence of both species illustrates the fact that human–machine relations are by no means free of emotional implications.

The Invaders' Invasion

"They become crazed, with eyes glazed, and are oblivious to everything around them." This is a statement not about the chronic hacker (sometimes known as the computer terminal case) but about those obsessed with the electronic game of Space Invaders. It was made by the British Member of Parliament George Foulkes when he led his campaign to curb "this menace" in 1981. His Control of Space Invaders (and Other Electronic Games) Bill was put before the House of Commons and was narrowly defeated, after a debate in which some members roundly condemned the leisure pursuit while others confessed to their own weakness for the game.

In the original version of Invaders the player shoots at little green space creatures who dance along a TV screen, dropping lethal bombs as they shuffle ever nearer. If they are all exterminated before the threatened landing, they are replaced by a further contingent of even more menacing aliens. The player cannot win but has to achieve the highest possible score before the inevitable defeat. A novice may lose three "lives" and perish within seconds, but the level of skill soon rises, and with it the excitement and the prospect of becoming hooked on the game. Those who eventually become indifferent to the standard green peril may go on to face the challenge of further threats of death or infestation by other cosmic or terrestrial beings. Phoenix involves colorful bombing birds that flap around menacingly and squawk pitifully when hit, and other terrors are presented by The Rats, The Killer Bees and The Ultra Moths. PAC-MAN ™ is a "muncher" not a "zapper"—he wanders through a maze gobbling up points and chasing "blue meanies." The video game industry is currently worth $6 billion a year and the games are becoming much more sophisticated, with 3-D graphics and "talk-back." In SPACE SPARTANS ™ a pleasant female voice provides helpful information while the voices of the aliens are menacing and male.

As far as most players are concerned, these games are simply innocent pastimes that provide excitement and a sense of satisfaction. The machines give added testimony to the fact that, with an imaginative style of presentation, computers have a lot to offer the wider public. The rapid proliferation of the games, and the rate at which new versions are being devised, also show how manufacturers eagerly respond to market demands. There are now about 100,000 public machines in Britain alone, and Americans spend well over $4 billion annually on these games. In addition, millions of chip-based devices are plugged regularly into domestic television sets.

So a significant proportion of the world's population is now in direct and interactive contact with computer-based systems and appears to derive considerable stimulation and pleasure from such encounters. In a minority of cases, however, it appears that the enjoyment of Invaders-type games can become a real addiction and can lead to serious problems. Children may miss school or shun their friends, preferring instead to thwart a cosmic attack, and a few have even resorted to crime to provide the necessary funds. Recent newspaper headlines tell of some unorthodox methods allegedly used by young people to finance their obsession. A thirteen-year-old girl turned to prostitution, a boy of the same age stole cash raised for his grandmother's funeral, and a seventeen-year-old youth blackmailed a vicar with whom he had formed a sexual liaison.

We may suspect that in some cases an addiction to the machine is falsely claimed in an attempt to lessen the blame. It gives a topical flavor to a plea of diminished responsibility, not for the first time placing computer systems in the role of scapegoat. Yet there is little doubt that electronic games can be seductive and can produce a kind of craving. During the game itself, strong feelings may be provoked, and more than one young person has had to receive hospital treatment for injuries received by attempting to repel the invaders with a well-aimed fist rather than with the electronic weaponry provided. In Japan, over 150 children have been taken into custody for offenses connected with electronic machines, and one couple, despairing of their addicted son, sent him to relatives in mainland China, one of the few remaining havens free from alien penetration.

It is unfortunate that the first major leisure use of computer technology should have resulted in a number of casualties, but it is clear that there has been a disproportionate amount of attention paid to such dramatic cases and that the large majority of enthusiasts remain happy, healthy, and nondeviant. There may be many cases in which the challenge of Invaders has promoted a new enthusiasm and increased self-respect and popularity. Certainly, for many young people it has provided at least a temporary relief from boredom.

It is to be regretted that the accent in most of the games is on shooting and aggression rather than on rescue and cooperation, but the flexible machine need not be used solely to encourage such negative tendencies. We can imagine endless possibilities for games that have some form of "helping" as their goal. Traffic Scout, for example, might introduce an endless stream of little old ladies requiring assistance to cross a busy street, or Lifeboat Rescue might encourage the player to pluck survivors from a hazardous sea. A range of challenging Surgery Simulations might allow the amateur surgeon to carry out electronic operations, while in Obstetric Obstacles the player might assist in countless difficult births, with each success rewarded by a high score and a healthy cry from a bonny electronic infant!

Many computer scientists, and most of the hackers, would look on such productions with great disdain—just as they do on any form of electronic game. Such trivia, they claim, is not the proper use for their hallowed technology. Yet computers have no rightful province, they belong nowhere and everywhere. Those who want to decomputerize society would be better off starting with the nuclear arsenals than with the amusement arcades. The use of high technology is no longer restricted to an elite, and Invader games, though of slight significance in many respects, demonstrate that this technology is easily "given away" and may have a powerful effect. Where the little green aliens have led, much more endearing and companionable creatures will surely follow.

Over the Barrier

The idea of an intimate relationship with a machine is at first sight preposterous, some would say obscene. We will explore the moral arguments later, but initially let us consider the evidence that shows that the idea is not as absurd as we might first imagine. We shall describe the widespread animism toward objects and consider the particular potency of computer programs a little later. However, it should be clear that while they may be written in such a way as to simulate human responses and encourage emotional involvement, in order to introduce such systems to a wide public the current antagonism, fear, and reservations toward computers will need to be overcome. There is a machine barrier, a reluctance to come to terms with computers, that will be crossed only when both hardware and software are more attractive, accessible, and approachable.

A number of programmers have already experimented with antihostility programs that are specially designed to win over the person who faces initial contact with the machine with antagonism and suspicion. Such programs recognize stereotyped replies to questions and respond with particular charm, humor, and good manners. The programming involved calls not for special technical wizardry but rather for social sensitivity and skill, and the most successful of these programs are very good indeed at making human friends and influencing people.

Another approach to crossing the barrier is through "softening" machines that are initially attractive because of their practicality. Calculators are highly functional and antagonize few people. Speaking calculators have now been introduced, and we can expect these to have a popular novelty value. From here it is a small step to a machine that speaks a greeting, and by this point people will be well on the way to accepting a two-way conversation device. We can anticipate a similar breakdown of reserve through the evolution of computer-based game machines. Some of these machines speak already, enticing the player into another game, and it cannot be long before some pregame repartee is possible.

The initial overcoming of the barrier, and the enjoyment that will come from interacting with the machine, will lay the foundation for the development of a social relationship. Programs will be written to "get to know" the person and to gradually increase the intimacy of the relationship. The techniques used will be based on the social skill of the programmer and on the structured knowledge about the nature of relationships that is available from social psychologists. Computers will be accepted as social beings because they are capable of producing cues that are essentially social in nature. They appear to be intelligent, for one thing, and they appear to be responsive, sometimes simulating great insight and sensitivity. The writer Studs Terkel has described the way in which people who are faced with a new experience search for some metaphor with which to understand it. The airplane is therefore "just like a bird," and we feel comfortable with such a homely analogy. The computer, if it is like anything, is like a person—it cannot as easily be reduced to any other "as if." It behaves as if it knows what it is doing, as if it is conscious, and as if it understands. We experience only the output, the machine's responses; the program and the mechanisms are hidden from us. It is little wonder that performances can be so impressive. The puppet appears to have no strings.

The attribution of personality to an intelligent and personal system is fully to be expected when we recall the animistic response to much humbler objects. If machines like the steam engine can elicit social feelings from some people, it is hardly surprising that far more sophisticated systems can promote relationships. When the factory robot "Clyde the Claw" broke down in Chicago recently, the workers sent it flowers and a get-

well-soon card. When systems are designed and programmed specifically to encourage social relationships,
the strength of feelings involved can hardly be imagined.

The Computer as Psychotherapist

Many of the most striking current examples of an emotional involvement with a computer program come from
the area of computer psychotherapy. When Joseph
Weizenbaum created ELIZA, he treated it as an exercise
in the illusion of natural conversation. He used the mode
of "nondirective counseling" simply because, for technical reasons, it was easier to implement this than the more
normal style of dialogue. He certainly did not mean the
program to be taken seriously as a therapist, and he was
surprised and somewhat horrified at the ease with which
ELIZA's "clients" became emotionally involved. He
wrote:

People who knew very well that they were conversing with a
machine soon forgot that fact, just as theatregoers, in the grip
of suspended disbelief, soon forget that the action they are
witnessing is not "real." . . . They would demand to be permitted to converse with the system in private and would, after
conversing with it for a little time, insist, in spite of my
explanations, that the machine really understood them.

In demonstrating ELIZA I have also been struck by
how seriously people take it. It asks a question, and they
think long and hard before providing a true and considered answer. They seem unwilling to treat the interaction merely as a game, and their answers are often so
intimate that the demonstrator prefers to withdraw and
leave them alone together. Weizenbaum suggested that
the adoption of what we have called the "fictional mode"
is more evident in the case of people who do not understand machine systems than with computer experts.
However, even those who have been involved in the
development of the program are not immune. Weizen-

baum's secretary, who had been with him through the creation of ELIZA, had no sooner started a conversation with the pilot version of the program than she asked her boss to leave the room.

Pamela McCorduck describes how she witnessed a conversation between an internationally known computer scientist and another of Weizenbaum's programs, DOCTOR. The eminent man began to disclose anxieties about his highly emotional relationship with his wife: "We watched in painful embarrassment, trying hard not to look, yet mesmerized at the same time. Something about the impartial machine had evoked a response from the visitor that the norms of polite human conduct forbade."

Weizenbaum was startled to see the degree of anthropomorphism his program elicited:

I knew of course that people form all sorts of emotional bonds to machines, for example to musical instruments, motorcycles, and cars. And I knew from long experience that the strong emotional ties many programmers have to their computers are often formed after only short exposures to their machines. What I had not realised is that extremely short exposures to a relatively simple computer program could induce powerful delusional thinking in quite normal people.

The strength of the effect raised doubts in Weizenbaum's mind as to the ethics of publishing such a program. It *was* published, however, and is now available worldwide. Simple versions are also available for use on home computers.

Given the powerful emotional responses which ELIZA and DOCTOR can evoke, it is not surprising that impressive claims are made for their therapeutic effectiveness. Weizenbaum himself makes no such claim. He has become thoroughly disenchanted with the intrusion of computers into areas that he now thinks ought to be the sole preserve of human social contacts. Nevertheless, others—psychologists and psychiatrists rather than computer scientists—have taken up his pioneering work and are busy applying his programs in clinical settings and developing therapeutic programs of their own. There is now considerable evidence that the animistic response is every bit as strong in the clinic as in the laboratory. Over half the clients who interacted with DOCTOR in a Massachusetts hospital insisted that they were conversing with a real person, although they had been told quite specifically that a computer was operating the terminal. Even when such animism does not occur, clients often say that they prefer interaction with the machine to that with a human therapist. Most people do not find the computer cold and impersonal, and many feel more at ease discussing highly personal topics with the machine.

Some of these programs can be seen as basically providing a structured means by which people can talk to themselves. Recent studies have shown that such an outlet can often have a beneficial effect even without the computer as an aid. In a procedure known as "McFall's Mystical Monitor," a person simply tape-records completely unstructured self-talk for an hour or so. After listening to the tape once through, it is erased, and then the whole procedure is repeated three or four times. For most people the initial unease and embarrassment is soon replaced by what they find to be a very constructive elaboration of ideas, an exploration of their feelings and attitudes. McFall's idea is similar to that used in a number of literary and dramatic productions including Samuel Beckett's *Krapp's Last Tape*.

Two psychotherapists, the brothers Charles and Warner Slack, have combined structured self-talk with a computer program modeled closely on their own interview style as therapists. At appropriate points in the conversation the computer asks: "Would you like to talk more about this?" and if the reply is "Yes" the client is instructed to talk into a tape-recorder that is automatically switched on. The program has been written to be especially warm and lifelike. When the person is speaking about a particular sadness, for example, the machine displays the message: "Good, we are listening to you talking about your sadness." In one of the Slacks' studies, clients received half of their therapy from one of the brothers and half from the computer, and they were then asked to compare the experiences. Overall there was a preference for the human therapist, although some clients actually favored the computer. While this study does not suggest that the program in question could adequately match the skills of the real counselor, it was found that clients generally reacted quite favorably to the machine. They often spoke to it frankly and emotionally about their problems, and several felt that it had helped them. Two clients who had recently lost someone very close to them confided in the computer but not in the human therapist.

Another approach to computer-based psychotherapy has recently been developed by Morton Wagman at the University of Illinois. His PLATO program is based on a form of therapy known as "dilemma counseling." Founded on the premise that most of the problems that people face can be stated in the form of a conflict between two or more different courses of action, the computer elicits such alternatives and then computes several ways in which the problem may be solved. There is thus more "thinking" by the machine in this system than in those that rely principally on the client's own expression of emotion. The computer using the PLATO program works out possible solutions to the client's problem by a complex logical method. It then provides active guidance and makes concrete suggestions. Nine out of ten of the students who used the system said that they found it helpful, and that the machine had suggested worthwhile and practical solutions. Less than one in three said that the computer was impersonal, and almost half said that they were more at ease than they would have been with a human therapist. There was also evidence from a follow-up that the system had in fact helped to reduce the number and severity of the problems which had been presented.

There are, of course, many brands of psychotherapy, and some lend themselves more readily to computer realization than others. Freudian psychoanalysis, for example, would be very difficult to operationalize on a machine, whereas the reflective method of Carl Rogers provided the inspiration for ELIZA and proved very suitable. Charles and Warner Slack use an amalgam of strategies from several therapists, and Morton Wagman has found it relatively easy to adapt his own dilemma-counseling system to program format. Different therapeutic approaches present the computer in a different way. In some, the personality of the machine is presented as particularly warm and encouraging, whereas in others it appears as a highly intellectual fact-finder. Where guidance and interpretation are given by the machine this can reflect any one of a range of underlying theories, and many alternative attitudes and implicit philosophies can be expressed. Russell Cassell's Computerized Pastoral Counseling System, for example, has a theoretical base in the Christian philosophy. Bizarre as it may seem, this Christian computer program bases its analysis and advice on the teachings of Jesus. We can envisage future Family Planning Programs available in optional Roman Catholic and Protestant versions.

Uses of the computer in the field of psychological therapy are not limited to counseling. For many years machines have been used to control the administration of mild anxiety-eliciting stimuli in the procedure known as "desensitization," which can be highly effective in treating phobias. They have also been programmed to stimulate play in autistic children, and in one study they were used to elicit speech in children suffering from a form of mutism. For each of these applications it has been claimed that the computer is a highly effective therapist.

In addition to the therapeutic role, machines are now used to administer medical interviews. The process by which a physician takes a history from a patient and collects information about symptoms is often a long and unsatisfactory one. Doctors have therefore cooperated with programmers in drawing up a framework of the ideal interview. The program includes many "branches" so that follow-up questions may be asked if a patient's response suggests that further probing is necessary. There are several important advantages to using a computer to conduct such an initial medical interview. It never omits a question, it has an unfailing memory for the answers that the patient gives, and it can provide a printed summary in a standard form. This provides the physician with a useful starting point for the consultation that follows. The process is very cheap, and it saves a lot of the doctor's time.

Several such interview systems have been developed, and it has been found that patients generally enjoy their interaction with the machine. Christopher Evans of the National Physical Laboratory at Teddington, near London, spent a number of years developing his interview program, MICKIE. A good deal of research went into the wording of the questions (avoiding the jargon and ambiguity of which physicians are often guilty) and into building a friendly personality into the machine. Animism was thus encouraged by this good-natured and nonpatronizing program, and most patients said that they preferred MICKIE to the traditional medical interview.

It appears that the computer is particularly appreciated where health enquiries relate to highly personal areas. Questions about sexual problems, gynecological health, and alcohol intake, for example, are answered without embarrassment and with more accuracy and frankness than in interpersonal interviews. Alcoholics responding to a specially written program in a Glasgow hospital, for example, admitted to drinking 50 percent more alcohol than when they were interviewed by consultants in the clinic. Another highly sensitive area is that of personal attitudes to suicide, and John Greist, a psychiatrist working on a Suicide Risk Prediction Project at the University of Wisconsin, has written a program that helps to identify people in danger of attempting to take their own lives. He has been able to show that in this context, too, the computer interview is able to provide a more accurate picture than that obtained during an interview with a skilled clinician.

Doctors who have used such programs have not only been favorably impressed with their usefulness, but have also often been surprised at how easily patients adapt to the machine. They also report a marked tendency to relate to the computer as if it were a person. It now seems highly likely that systems such as the ones we have described will be increasingly employed in the clinical setting. There are a number of other ways in which computers can be used as medical aids, and some of these could benefit from becoming humanized. Nurses have reported that patients in intensive-care units sometimes develop a kind of psychological dependence on the computerized systems that constantly monitor their functions. They become adept at interpreting the readings and feel happy that the machine is watching over them. These machines could of course be made much friendlier, providing verbal feedback to the patient about his or her condition. A speech that runs: "Well, John, your blood pressure's just a little high; I think I'll call the nurse. Nothing for you to worry about," would cause the patient far less alarm than ringing bells and flashing emergency lights.

There are several medical programs in which the professional, rather than the patient, interacts with the machine. Some doctors now employ computers as resident consultants to help them in the diagnosis of difficult cases. A program developed for use by nurses screens for high-risk pregnancies, and another is used by radiologists. The interpretation of X-ray images is a complex skill that needs the educated eye of the highly trained human, but computerized image-analysis techniques and knowledgeable programs can be used interactively by the radiologist to help in decision-making.

At this stage in time there is no question of the computer supplanting the physician or the psychiatrist, but sophisticated machines do have a wide variety of uses in the clinical setting.

The Computer as Teacher

The computer is as good at providing information as it is at eliciting it. We are already surrounded by numerous sources of information, but, unlike the book and the television set, the appropriately programmed machine is able to tailor its presentation to the individual needs of a student. Computer terminals linked into major systems will ultimately provide a perfect reference service, bringing global knowledge resources to the researcher's desk. Machines can also act as elementary-level teachers, feeding information to the learner at a suitable pace. The size of the learning steps can be made dependent on the student's previous responses, and where problems do occur the machine can slow down, providing extra examples and explaining the material in greater depth. Thus the precise course that the machine takes through the program will reflect the student's abilities and relative strengths and weaknesses. The computer never becomes impatient, and it never tires, becomes angry, or makes a mistake. It never has an off-day and has no favorites.

A distinction is sometimes made between "computer-assisted instruction," in which the emphasis is on the provision of information according to a preset format, and "computer-assisted learning," in which the course of a program run is highly dependent upon the feedback from the student. The computer may be no match for the gifted individual tutor, but such a luxury is available to few, and the machine can provide a good standard of individual teaching within the framework of the normal classroom. So far, teaching programs do not attempt to understand the learner and cannot react appropriately to wide-ranging questions, but the most advanced systems incorporate artificial intelligence techniques and allow the student to learn by a flexible discovery method. A wide variety of programs have been designed, covering many subjects and all levels of ability from the preschool to the postgraduate. The evidence suggests that such programs can provide highly effective instruction. Moreover, students enjoy using them; they find them fun, and they relate to the machines in many ways as if they were human teachers.

Teaching programs and the machines that present them are frequently designed to encourage animism. LEACHIM, for example, is a system that has been teaching for over ten years in a New York school. The computer has a face and arms and can recognize each of the children in the class by the analysis of speech patterns. The nine- and ten-year-olds who are taught science, history, mathematics, and social studies by the machine tend to become personally involved with it. According to Michael Freeman, the teacher who wrote the program, "the kids love the machine," and he has arranged that children who perform especially well be periodically rewarded with one of LEACHIM's jokes or poems. Similar projects have now been developed by several other schools. At Lowbrook School in Berkshire, England, a computer teaches spelling and mathematics to five- to eleven-year-olds. Correct answers are praised and the child's own name is used. Not surprisingly the children wait impatiently for their turn on the machine, and they are said to treat it like a friendly teacher. They have also provided it with a wig to make it look more human.

LOGO is a system that originated in the artificial intelligence laboratory at the Massachusetts Institute of Technology. The "main brain" is located at MIT and is linked to several terminals in local schools. The first lesson presented to the children involves geometry, but it is disguised as "the turtle game." Little humpbacked creatures can be ordered, via the terminal, to move in any direction across a sheet of paper laid on the floor. As they crawl around they leave a trail drawn by a pen attached to their underside. The turtle shape encourages animism, operating it is fun, and the children enjoy the feeling of control. The lessons available include biology, languages, and music, and the children are encouraged to explore new possibilities for themselves. The accent, then, is on discovery rather than on the formal presentation of information. By inventing projects of their own, the children become explorers within the various realms of knowledge offered by the program, while at the same time they become used to the idea of manipulating a computer keyboard, and many gain a new self-confidence through their relationship with the machine.

LOGO's creator, Seymour Papert, says: ". . . we are fundamentally concerned with creating a computer presence . . . which is resonant with people's sense of who they are and what they want to be." Teaching machines have sometimes been seen as inflexible tools for feeding predigested facts to children. With imagination and creative programming, however, computer-aided learning can be both flexible and demanding. It can also be fun. The computer can therefore provide a resource with which the child explores the world of knowledge; it does not have to be a machine for processing children. Young people typically respond with great enthusiasm to such systems. A program that provides frequent surprises, fun captions, cartoon graphics, and funny noises can transform the educational computer into the best toy in the world. Educationalists stress that constructive play can be a highly effective medium for learning, and computer manufacturers have already taken account of this in their production of microchip toys and games that encourage the child to spell accurately or perform increasingly difficult mathematical tasks. It is hardly surprising that these brightly colored playmates are often preferred to the classroom teacher.

Younger children, especially, are greatly stimulated by the additional cues to animism and may quickly develop an attachment to the responsive, playful object. I have watched a six-year-old girl showing her doll how the computer operates and explaining that it is a friend. There is something a little unnerving about a young child assuring a piece of plastic that a metal machine is a playmate, and the scene is particularly interesting because it shows an age-old form of animism side by side with the new electronic version. However, computer-based animism seems to persist long after dolls have been discarded. Teachers have often expressed surprise at the personalities that older children attribute to classroom computers, although some youngsters adopt another kind of attitude and become fascinated with the possibilities offered by programming. Mini-hackers have been known to spend several weeks developing computer-realizations of games they have invented or writing teaching aids for younger children.

A number of programs have been developed to help children with special needs, and once again it is evident that greater success is achieved when the machine is presented as a friend and when the learning is treated as a game. British psychologists working in Cambridge, for example, have developed a system that enables even profoundly deaf children to learn to speak clearly. A letter or word is first indicated to the child and the correct pronunciation is then shown on a TV screen. The display takes the form of a curve that is a visual analogy of the target sound. The child tries to match this with a curve produced by speaking into a microphone connected to the computer. Each attempt is awarded a number of points, and when a direct hit is scored added encouragement is given by a TV image of a teddy bear that gives a broad smile. According to one of the research workers, Edith Gulian, the children "love the game," and even two-year-olds have used the system, which can be based in the home, with great success, learning to speak in a way which is perfectly intelligible. Computer-controlled learning systems clearly have a great deal to offer to children with various forms of handicap.

Computer-aided learning is not just for children. Highly advanced systems instruct university students in electronic fault-finding and medical diagnosis, for example, and others are used to update the knowledge of working scientists and physicians. Such programs provide structured information and dispense with the fairground features that grip the attention of young children, but they do often have an easy conversational style and encourage a social form of interaction. There is obviously great potential for adult learning using such programs, and many different subject areas are currently being explored. Machine-aided language learning has received particular attention. Chris Evans' machine MINNIE provides a French–English dictionary and can test the user's vocabulary. There are also several commercial translation machines, some of which incorporate a voice synthesizer so that the foreign words and phrases can be heard as well as seen.

The software available for home computers already

includes programs that teach chess, mathematics, and science, but the huge potential market will be penetrated only if the learning experience is seen to be enjoyable. The machine becomes a more effective teacher if it is friendly, approachable, reinforcing, and easy to use; thus manufacturers and academic researchers are now beginning to examine those features that make machines and programs inviting and accessible to the nonspecialist.

Some of the results of such research are predictable. People like visual displays, preferably in color, and they also enjoy a variety of sounds. Synthesized speech adds greatly to involvement. Users also like to feel they have some degree of control, and prefer a machine that is obviously responding to them rather than one that appears to run a predetermined course. The timing of the machine's reactions can also be important. The computer is able to process information so quickly that the next step of a program will often be available for display immediately after the person has pressed a key. It may be more impressive, however, if the programmer inserts a slight pause so that the response time of the machine replicates the rhythm of human interaction. Just as children's programs are reinforced by jokes and funny noises, it seems that adult programs profit from more sophisticated forms of encouragement. In a study at the University of Southern California, William Sacks programmed a computer to give remedial spelling lessons. The machine responded differently to three groups of students, providing additional comments that were designed to represent a low, medium, or high level of social reinforcement. The study showed that the users who had received the maximum degree of reinforcement developed a more positive attitude to the machine and found the learning experience more enjoyable.

Donald Broadbent, leading a team of psychologists at Oxford University, developed a program in which a computer presented one of nine possible personalities.

The human subject who interacted with the machine chose an initial level of intimacy from very rude to loving, and from then on the computer and the user took turns in choosing from the twelve possible intimacy levels. Although the procedure was highly artificial, the subjects generally found it pleasurable and realistic, and the task provided a simulation of the growth of a relationship. The various personalities built into the program had different response tendencies, some reacting markedly to the human input and some taking little or no account of it. Some moved toward less intimacy, whereas others were predisposed to become affectionate.

The effects on the human subject varied with the personality presented by the machine. Some personalities were seen as more realistic, or humanlike, than others and such naturalness was positively associated with enjoyment. However, the machine's attempt to constantly increase the level of intimacy was not guaranteed to produce a pleasurable response to the user. It seemed as if pressure toward friendliness from the machine was acceptable only if it built upon the participant's own responses. This suggests that a computer may spoil the relationship if it appears to be too ingratiating, and that the optimal program should be sensitive to the level of intimacy implied by the person's own input. The dynamics of intimacy between the human and the machine will be a fascinating area for future study, and it may turn out that the most satisfying and lasting relationships are those that evolve toward greater affection in a gradual fashion. Broadbent's study also took account of the personality of the human user, and it was found that extroverts tended to respond with greater intimacy toward the machine than did introverts.

The Oxford study developed out of a project in which the computer was used as a tool to examine how business managers make decisions. The incidental observation that subjects tended to relate to the machine in a surprisingly personal way provided the inspiration for the intimacy experiment. Other studies of computer–human relationships, however, have their origins in social psychology. They have thus employed conceptual frameworks and methods that were first developed for the analysis of person-to-person interactions. Research by Richard Muller of Syracuse University used such a social psychological approach to examine social influence by a machine. Muller found that subjects' attitudes were changed in the same way when they heard a computer's opinion as when they heard the same opinion expressed by a fellow human. He was also able to show that if subjects had some familiarity with the machine and had previous experience of conversing with it, then the computer's power to influence their attitudes increased.

This research highlights a number of important points. The machine is not necessarily a purveyor of factual information; it can also express opinions, and these can affect human attitudes. It can be programmed to convey impressions, personal views, and propaganda, and can provide misinformation and lies just as easily as truths. It would be wrong, therefore, to see the machine as a fundamentally neutral instructor. We have already introduced the notion of the Christian computer, and a machine can be equally "committed" to any other moral or political system. There is a high credibility factor associated with the computer, and the experience of interacting with it may further increase its powers of persuasion. The technically sophisticated might be less credulous, but it seems that even the computer expert is not immune to the charm of some programs and can become deeply involved with psychotherapeutic and chess-playing systems. Another aspect of this influence is illustrated by the hacker's infatuation. Familiarity with a machine, it appears, does not necessarily breed contempt.

The studies that have been discussed reveal some of the social elements that would need to be incorporated in the optimal teaching machine. It would be responsive, reinforcing, and realistic. Features based on the best human teachers would be simulated, and the machine would take on a presence, have a personality, and become a character. It would, in a word, lend itself to animism. There is now abundant evidence, from the classroom, the laboratory, and the clinic, that people *do* often treat the machine as if it were a person. In the case of children, this response style may be based on a total delusion. For adults, the personhood of the machine is properly understood as a fiction, but it is a fiction that is easily accepted and much enjoyed.

Computers still have the image of distant forbidding machines, yet there are many ways in which they can be made softer and more approachable. If they are to be introduced on a mass scale into homes as teachers and social contacts, then their friendliness as well as their usefulness has to be emphasized. Those features that at present tend to alienate the uninitiated will have to be modified. Machines don't have to be austere and threatening, even if their functioning does depend on high technology. Despite initial fears and prejudices, television has now become fully accepted in most homes and has lost much of its image as a technological miracle. It has also had an effect on family interaction, providing an extension of shared experience while at the same time reducing the amount of person-to-person communication. Parents rate babysitting as one of the main uses of the television set, and one research worker has described it as a child's "electronic peer . . . the accessible playmate for the passive child." The home computer is also destined to be a focus for shared experience, but it is likely to stimulate interaction and discourage passivity. Unlike the TV, the machine will present a personality of its own, thus becoming a new family member. The electronic pet may nudge its way, affectionately and strategically, into a position of respect and influence.

Alan Turing and the Cues for Confusion

If a machine can convey the impression that it is a living and thinking being with a personality of its own, might there not come a point where there is a real confusion between machines and people?

British mathematician Alan Turing suggested that if a human being were unable, in a conversational test, to distinguish between a person and a machine, then we would have to conclude that the machine was thinking. Turing's criterion therefore relied not on objective performance but on whether the judge was convinced by the human impression conveyed by the machine throughout all attempts to reveal its true nature. He argued that if, under such test conditions, the computer remained indistinguishable from the human operator, it would have to be credited with the ability to think.

Under normal conditions, appearance and voice cues would immediately give the game away, and, since these have nothing to do with the thinking capacity of a system, Turing was concerned to eliminate any effects of such features. To do this he proposed that the test should take place under special conditions. The judge would be placed in a room with two computer terminals, one operated by a person in another room and one linked directly to a computer. The judge would be allowed to converse with each terminal on any topic and would eventually have to make a decision about which one was computer-operated. If the judgment was wrong, or if no firm decision could be made, then this result would indicate that the machine had passed the test. The rules of the proposed game allowed both the computer and the human operator to tell lies; the conversation could range over any area, and it would have to continue for as long as the judge wanted.

No existing program can pass the Turing test. As yet, no system has a sufficiently flexible understanding of language, and no program contains sufficient knowledge of the world to be able to converse on as wide a range of topics as a human being. It is worth remembering that even if a program of sufficient power were available it would have to be suitably tailored to the Turing task. It would have to be written to lie about certain matters, and some artificial limitations would have to be imposed. The machine would have to take its time, for example, over problems to which it would have an immediate answer (like the square root of 7483) and would have to act dumb about those things that most humans would not be expected to know. A superefficient machine would be instantly recognizable and would, strictly speaking, fail the test. We can see how such a high level of performance would produce an inadequate simulation of human responses, although it might seem unfair to judge that it had failed as a thinking machine simply because it was, in effect, thinking too fast.

Turing's test relies fundamentally on psychological impact. It can be criticized as an appropriate test for a thinking machine but is very useful as a test of human realism. For this reason it has a special importance in the animistic context. It would seem to be an elementary psychological truth that if two things cannot be told apart, then they will be treated in the same way. However, the Turing situation, with its emphasis on the reduction of peripheral cues such as those of voices and appearance, would be expected to produce only a fraction of the potential impact of artificial systems. The most sophisticated superbrain, operating via a terminal, might be far less impressive than a more meager intellect presented in realistic human form. The strength of reaction to puppets and dolls supports this idea, and, although at first glance such evidence might seem to be of little relevance to those involved in the development of computer systems, we have every reason to suppose that the overall impact of their devices in the field of social interaction will be greatly influenced by such additional cues.

Meanwhile, there is strong evidence that even interaction via terminals can lead people to project a personality onto the machine. Psychotherapeutic, teaching, and interview programs are all said to convey a human presence, and, because a certain amount of flexibility and randomness can be built into programs, even the people who have developed them are not immune to such feelings. Describing this phenomenon, Chris Evans wrote, "I have had the same spooky experience . . . when chatting with computers I have programmed myself, and often find their answers curiously perceptive and unpredictable." In all of these situations the effect is produced despite the fact that the person *knows* that he or she is conversing with an artificial system. When this belief is not present then the effects can be dramatic.

Daniel Bobrow was a senior computer scientist working for a large American corporation. To allow him to work at home as well as in his office, a computer link was installed in his house so that Bobrow could gain access to the central machine at any time. Messages could be relayed between the two locations, and the facility could therefore be used as a telephone, except, of course, that the conversations were typed rather than spoken. Late one night the vice-president of the company needed to pass an urgent message to the computer expert, and, finding that the central terminal was still operating, he typed in a greeting. A reply soon came, and the boss therefore imagined that the conscientious employee was still hard at work. The nature of the reply, however, struck him as a little strange. This was hardly surprising, since Bobrow had gone to bed and the computer was operating a psychotherapeutic program. The questions that the vice-president continued to ask were not therefore given direct answers, but produced non-committal replies of the "Why do you ask?" variety.

After a number of attempts to get a straight answer, the executive became angry and typed in a suitable rebuke. The program's cool, reflective reply did nothing to soothe the situation, and after further interchanges of a similar kind the highly irritated man phoned the house to continue the argument at a greater pace. A sleepy Daniel Bobrow, roused from his bed, was at first shocked by the irate tones of the employer but soon realized what had happened and started to laugh loudly. The outraged boss took a lot of convincing before accepting that he had spent several minutes arguing with a machine.

Stories such as this vividly illustrate the confusion potential of current programs. The Bobrow situation was unusual because the context cues produced entirely the wrong set of expectations. However, most people who interact with a terminal *know* that they are conversing with a program, and, despite this, the machine's reactions can still suggest a human presence. We now have evidence of this effect from laboratory research, from classrooms, and from clinics. Turing's test may provide the ultimate criterion, but it is clearly not necessary to develop the perfect Turing program before some degree of illusion is produced. We now have a good idea of many of the features of conversational style that can add realism to a program and increase people's enjoyment of interaction with the machine. Yet while the development of such interactional programs is likely to focus on increasing the psychological impact of computers, by improving the use of such conversational cues, it would be a mistake to ignore the peripheral features of appearance, voice, and movement. These have been shown to have profound effects on inducing animism toward less sophisticated objects, and they will add much to the social power of computer systems.

CHAPTER 4
Animism

Animism

"People see the world not as it is but as they are." There is a tendency to interpret the appearance and behavior of animals and physical objects in essentially human terms. The camel looks like a haughty person, the fox seems cunning. We may regard the family dog as an almost human character who understands people's feelings, and even the humble canary may be seen as having complex insights into human affairs and a personality of its own.

But the tendency to personify extends to nonliving things too. The wind may sound angry, the sea may be cruel. We may become attached to personal possessions, regarding them as old friends. The family car may be given a nickname, and a man may regard his favorite pipe as a close friend. Sailing ships and steam engines seem particularly powerful in fostering affection. People will sometimes try to persuade or encourage mechanical contrivances to work properly by talking or shouting at them. They may feel that the machine is being willful and stubborn. "It won't work," they say. "It simply refuses."

In such familiar experiences we get a glimpse of a deeply entrenched psychological disposition. In certain circumstances people will respond to an inanimate object as if it were living. Given special cues, they will establish relationships with machines and other artifacts and will react as if they were encountering another human being. We have a strong disposition to recognize the human characteristics of nonhuman objects. Emotional feelings, which are generally a response to social situations, may be stimulated by pieces of wood, lumps of clay, or suitably engineered machinery. This curious effect will be powerfully elicited by a new generation of intelligent, friendly, and even lovable computers. The basic readiness to react in such a way, however, has long been studied and discussed by anthropologists and psychologists, who label it animism.

Artists and entertainers have capitalized on this tendency for many centuries. Cleverly produced and manipulated artifacts are prized for their lifelike quality. Dolls and religious statues are often produced in such a way that the artist strives to blur the distinction between the image and that which it represents. In portraits and waxworks the aim is to capture a true likeness and portray character, so that a total impression of the subject is conveyed. The most effective artistic productions make us feel that we are in the presence of an actual person. It is as if they might come alive and step out of the canvas.

The potential confusion between the image and the reality it represents has been the theme of numerous fantasies portrayed in novels, ballets, films, and poems. In these the artist's fiction that the object lives becomes a fact within the drama. The ventriloquist's dummy speaks of its own accord, the wooden puppet becomes flesh and blood, the portrait changes as the person portrayed becomes mad or bad. It is a common theme, repeated through many centuries and across many cultures. There is a deeply held fascination that may well have its origins in a primitive and universal psychological process. By understanding the nature of this process, we may find important clues about how the qualities of computer-based artifacts may be optimized so that they will transcend their true inanimate nature and promote the illusion of life and personality. By examining certain facets of the mental life of primitive peoples and of young children, we may glimpse the origins of this pervasive and potentially critical confusion between the living world and the inanimate.

Primitive Roots

At one time anthropologists regarded animism as a universal characteristic of the primitive mind. Andrew Lang spoke of the tendency as ". . . that inextricable confusion in which man, beasts, plants, stones and stars are all on one level of personality and animated existence." In *The Golden Bough* Sir James Frazer provided a rich tapestry of illustrations of animism from many diverse cultures. "To the savage," he wrote, "the world in general is animate, and trees and plants are no exception to the rule. He thinks that they have souls like his own and treats them accordingly." Rice, corn, and trees have frequently been regarded as conscious, and in some cultures it was the practice to address a tree with a ritual prayer, begging its forgiveness before axing it or plucking its fruit. Certain tribal groups, however, were less deferential and would threaten the vegetation with destruction unless it bore a good crop. As late as the nineteenth century, according to Frazer, it was a common practice among European peasants to mimic scything before cabbages that were curling their leaves rather than forming heads. It was fervently hoped that this would intimidate the vegetables and thus persuade them to correct their growth.

Another practice that illustrates animism is the punishing of lifeless objects. If we trip over a stool we may kick it angrily in retaliation, and we may blame tools for a faulty job, as if they were being deliberately unhelpful. Sometimes such remonstrations and punishments are more formal. Aristotle, for example, chronicled the judicial trials of lifeless objects in Greece. In the Athenian ritual known as "the murder of the ox," the axe and the knife that the slaughterers had wielded during the sacrificial act were given a mock trial. They were invariably found guilty and were condemned and thrown into the sea. Even civilized legal codes retain remnants of such practices. Until recently the law of New Jersey ordered that any car which had been involved in a fatal accident must be destroyed, and international maritime law allows for ships to be arrested. The issue of the status of physical objects in the legal and moral domain has been seriously discussed in recent years by philosophers, and some of them have come to the conclusion that sophisticated "robot-persons" would have to be accorded certain civil rights and held to have some responsibility for their actions. It might seem a bizarre idea to have an inanimate object standing trial in court, but clearly this would not be something entirely new in human legal practice.

There are several explanations of the origins of animism. Some anthropologists have suggested that it helped to provide reassurance that the physical world was friendly and possessed a conscience. Others have suggested that animism is a direct consequence of a basic human religious inclination by which soul or spirit is universally sought and universally found. The German psychologist Wilhelm Wundt favored such a view and suggested that ". . . primitive animism may be looked upon as the spiritual expression of man's natural state." According to another school of thought, people need to identify with everything around them, and animism stems from an all-embracing parallel drawn between the self and other things. In *The Natural History of Religion*, published in 1757, the philosopher David Hume made exactly this point. "There is a universal tendency among mankind," he wrote, "to conceive all beings like themselves and to transfer to every object those qualities with which they are intimately acquainted and of which they are intimately conscious." Similarly, the present day psychologists Charles Cofer and Mortimer Appley state that animism ". . . refers to the tendency of people to think of animals and aspects of inanimate nature, like clouds and the wind, for example, as possessing a soul and as being moved by purposes, wishes and motives that are similar to those which people see in themselves."

A variation on this view suggests that objects are seen as having feelings and personality not because they are "just like me" but because they are "just like you." Some psychologists believe that we are biologically predisposed to seek out and recognize other members of our species. As a social animal the human being is always looking for signs of other people, and, the argument runs, this tendency is so comprehensive and so powerful that it spills over from the appropriate domain and leads us to falsely identify lifeless objects as persons.

While these various explanations differ in several respects, they do share the idea that animism reflects a natural psychological predisposition. Animism and the related concepts "anthropomorphism" and "personification" are thus seen as having a universal relevance, and such a view clearly implies that even today people do not see the material world as entirely lifeless. If we are generally not aware of our own animistic thinking, then this is because the contemporary cultural climate controls such effects by emphasizing the rational and the scientific and discrediting the mystical and the imaginative. But there is ample evidence that the tendency persists, largely dormant but still readily evoked in the presence of suitable stimuli. Such stimuli include many, like puppets and dolls, that have amused and captivated people for centuries, but there are also new presentations that have been made possible by recent advances in art and technology. Objects may now be produced that sharply reawaken the potential for animistic thinking, and it now seems probable that the force of this ancient predisposition is about to reach new heights. Technology now has the power to ensure that we are confused by physical objects, confused into thinking that they have feelings and motives. Animism will ensure that computers are regarded as having personality. They will be made to perform in such a way that we will be forced to admit that they have presence, personality, and charisma.

How Children See Things

Children's minds are different from those of adults. To the young child, an object which has disappeared from view no longer exists, a frog may turn into a prince, and a conjurer really does have the power to cut ladies harmlessly in half and to charm solid balls from thin air. Animism is a prominent feature of the magical thinking of young children. They readily ascribe feelings, thoughts, and motives to all manner of inanimate objects. In an autobiographical fragment Dudley Kidd wrote, "I remember as a child feeling sorry for stones, feeling that they must get very tired of looking at the same objects every day; so I used to turn them over or throw them over the hedge so that they would get a new outlook."

Social scientists have now carried out systematic studies of childhood animism, and much of what we know about the subject comes from the work of the Swiss psychologist Jean Piaget. Through his careful games and discussions with children of many ages, Piaget was able to discover the criteria by which things are considered to be "alive" and "conscious," and to describe the changes which take place in children's thinking styles as they get older. Up to the age of about six years all things are considered to be conscious. A two-year-old explained to Piaget that there weren't any boats on the lake because "They're asleep," and a three-year-old was puzzled when a train had been missed. She asked, "Doesn't the train know that we're not on it?" Young children also make moral judgments about physical things. A ball may be regarded as "wicked" for leaping over a fence, and a rug that trips people is a "naughty" rug. Toward the end of this first stage children question their earlier assumptions and make inquiries about the distinction between the inanimate and the animate. One child asked Piaget, "Why don't stones die like insects when you put them in a box?" and another asked, "Does it hurt food when you eat it?"

Piaget showed that, after the age of six, movement is taken to be the prime criterion of life. Although stationary objects are now seen as dead, anything that changes position is regarded as living. Movement is taken as evidence of consciousness and intention. A wound-up string untwists itself because it wishes to. It feels uncomfortable and wants to unwind. Later a distinction is made between movement imposed on an object and that which is spontaneous. Clouds may therefore be seen as living, and if the child is told that they are blown by the wind then it is assumed that it is the wind which has life. There are clear parallels between childhood animism and that which has been described by anthropologists as a feature of adult thinking among primitive peoples. It involves not the playful use of deliberate fiction, but rather a natural and genuine system of beliefs about the world.

From about the age of twelve years children generally come to apply the concept of life only to animals and plants. This change in their understanding comes about partly as a consequence of their direct experience of the world and partly as a result of education by adults and older children. The degree of animism that survives can be measured, and in a recent study by Robert Billingham and Victoria Fu it was shown that this is related to the degree of animism which persists in the mother's thinking style. It has also been found with older children that those who come from a highly religious background tend to have a high score on tests of animism.

Many adult influences actually encourage children to personify animals and machines. Cartoon films frequently feature cats and canaries, rabbits and broomsticks, houses and cars that clearly exhibit all the signs of life and understanding. Similarly, stories attach unmistakably human features to all manner of physical objects and creatures. Railway engines have long been a favorite target for such characterization, and the Reverend William Awdry, for example, has written over twenty books portraying endearing animated engines that can think for themselves and talk together. His titles include such favorites as *James the Red Engine* and *Gordon the Big Engine*. Today's diesels seem not to lend themselves as readily to such humanization, and other types of machines have now been groomed for stardom. One recent successful example of automobile personification is Walt Disney's Herbie, the Volkswagen with a mind of its own. Adults often find these stories and films amusing, too, for animism persists in some form long after the days of childhood have ended.

And Adults Too

There is also an adult literature in which physical objects appear as living characters. In Rudyard Kipling's poem *007*, for example, a young railway engine achieves acceptance by his elders only after successfully proving himself by an act of heroism. In Victorian times coins, stamps, and pocket watches "wrote autobiographies" with titles such as *The Memoirs of a Guinea,* in which the object, having passed through many human hands, disclosed details of the affairs which it had witnessed. The extremes of literary output at that time were such that while half of these publications were written with a high moralistic outlook, the other half were frank sexual exposés designed to cater to "the other Victorians."

There is a familiar adult willingness to playfully indulge in such animistic fantasies, but in certain circumstances a full-blown delusional animism may return in maturity. Old people suffering from a severe senile condition may display a childlike animism, and schizophrenia may give rise to delusions and hallucinations in which physical objects come alive. Buildings, furniture, and electronic apparatus may be attributed with consciousness and the ability to read thoughts. In the most famous literary example of disturbed thought processes leading to profound animism, Don Quixote imagined that windmills were giant foes and that their sails were flailing arms. The normal constraint of adult thinking styles may also be weakened by the use of certain drugs. In *The Variety of Psychedelic Experience* Robert Masters and Jean Houston describe how a person experiencing the effects of LSD may develop an "empathic relationship" with a stone, imagining that there is "real understanding between the two of them."

In contrast to such rare and extreme effects, nondelusional animism, the "playful fiction" that inanimate objects think and feel, is very widespread. In a recent review of scientific studies of animism in adults, the psychologists William Looft and Wayne Bartz concluded that this mode of thinking is almost universal across agegroups and cultures. Nearly twenty years ago Leonard Brown and Robert Thouless asked people for a list of nonliving things that they sometimes responded to as if they were alive. The final list included dolls, idols, statues of saints, photographs, paintings, and prized possessions such as cars and boats. There is no doubt that in recent years computers have also come to merit a place in such a catalog. There is, however, a considerable difference between the animism of childhood and that of intelligent, nondeluded adults. It is not that adults are unable, as children are, to correctly distinguish between the living and the nonliving, but rather that in certain circumstances they choose to waive their normal rational mode of thinking.

A common motive for entering into an animistic fiction is that of wanting to play or wanting to be entertained. Testimony to the fact that adults find the personification of the physical world attractive and entertaining comes from the frequent use of "object characters" in advertising material and executive toys. A few years ago an American company marketed the highly successful Pet Rock. This consisted of nothing more than a round stone presented in a plush box described as its luxury home. The plaything came with full instructions for the care of the pet, and the owner was reminded to be considerate toward the stone and to take its feelings into account at all times. Many who received such rocks as gifts must have felt more than a twinge of ambivalence about their new friend, but some at least showed a readiness and ability to enter into the spirit of make-believe. Similarly, when we are successfuly entertained by puppets, we suspend our awareness of the real physical nature of the marionette and accept it instead as a little person within the fiction being presented. Thus, the psychological tendency that has received much attention as an aspect of the so-called primitive mentality and of the magical thinking of young children has a direct parallel in the experience of contemporary sophisticated adults.

Lively Shadows

Experiments have also shown that the latent animistic tendency is significant, universal, and surprisingly easily evoked. As we might expect from our understanding of children's criteria for life, a fundamental feature of many such demonstrations is movement that appears to be autonomous. In the early 1940s, the Belgian psychologist Albert Michotte examined the "perceptual tendency" of interpreting simple moving configurations in terms of cause and effect. He arranged for a colored square to move across a screen. When it came near another square it stopped abruptly and the second square moved sharply in the same direction. By a process of trial and error he found appropriate adjustments that made it appear as if there had been a collision between the squares. Michotte found that as well as this billiard-ball effect he could also produce a "pushcart" illusion or make it seem as if two objects had crashed and become welded together. He concluded that there was a primitive and universal tendency to see certain patterns of relative movement as action and reaction. There was, he said, a "causal illusion." Inferences are made beyond the information actually contained in the display, and people actively fill in information gaps to construct a plausible account of what is going on. According to Michotte, this is not a conscious process; human beings are predisposed to interpret certain displays in certain ways.

Michotte was also able to show that his moving displays produced another kind of interpretation. He noticed that his subjects tended to describe the kinetic patterns in human terms. Rapid contact between the shapes was seen as "violent" and slower movements were described as "gentle." Observers even attributed motives and intentions to the shapes. Depending on the type of movement, they might be labeled as friendly or aggressive.

At about the same time as Michotte was examining this curious phenomenon in Europe, two American psychologists, Fritz Heider and Marianne Simmel, were conducting experiments in which subjects were shown short animated films in which simple geometric shapes moved around the screen. The observers were invited to interpret what they saw taking place, and again they spontaneously endowed the figures with human characteristics. Depending on the speed and pattern of movement the shapes were described as "dancing together," "chasing one another," or "having a fight." A large triangle that appeared to push a circle around the screen was described as "warlike," "quarrelsome," "mean," and "quick to take offense." It was also dubbed "a bully" and "a villain."

Such demonstrations reveal how easily people are led to apply social judgments even when, as in the case of moving abstract shapes, they are utterly inappropriate. It is little wonder that with carefully contrived patterns that unmistakably portray "character," as in animated films, dramatic effects can be produced. Some of the observers in Heider and Simmel's study felt themselves becoming angry at the "viciousness" of the "bullying" triangle and were full of pity for the "poor little circle." This inherent reaction style may be fully exploited by the fine art of the caricaturist and the animator's skill for producing exquisitely timed movements. Cartoon films have the power to evoke, both in adults and in children, the full range of social emotions, from love to hate and from horror to pity. The curious fact is that such feelings are a response to moving lines and patches of color on the screen, and that the older spectators, at least, are perfectly well aware that the display is not "real." Artists play on this effect with sensational results, but it can also be seen to some degree with simple moving shapes. It would seem that even when cues of humanness are minimal, the tendency to animism may be in action, seeking out evidence of character and feeling.

Emotion and Form

Animism is predominantly a style of thinking, but it may thus form the basis for sentiments and emotions. Some feelings may be evoked through such an identification of an object as living, but it has also been suggested that there are patterns, sounds, and shapes that have a more direct effect in stimulating an emotional response. Some zoologists maintain that we are biologically preprogrammed to react to certain stimuli. In his book *Love and Hate,* the biologist Irenaus Eibl-Eibesfeldt suggests that people are predisposed to respond affectionately and protectively toward the young of many species because they bear what he calls "the hallmarks of cuddliness." With a relatively large head, big eyes, and chubby cheeks, they possess a certain cuteness that has universal appeal. He also suggests that artists and dollmakers have an implicit knowledge of this effect and stress such features when they want to produce an endearing physical object.

Sounds may also evoke feelings directly or through identification with human noises. Playing with a music synthesizer, we may produce a number of sound patterns that appear to have a certain meaning or that seem to create in us a particular emotional state. We now live in a world that has high music density, and we are surrounded by artificial and composed sounds. However, it seems likely that some of the effect has a more ancient origin and may be linked to our biological heritage.

Other emotional effects, however, probably arise from an identification of the stimulus pattern with some human characteristic. This recognition of the humanlike quality of nonhuman objects is the key feature of animism. Many years ago, the psychologist Theodore Lipps suggested that we find emotional expression in the inanimate because of a basic "empathic appreciation." Our animism leads us to have empathy with everything around us, and because of its influence the weeping willow may look sad, the towering building may look magnificent or threatening, and a broken chair may look as if it is in pain.

Seeking Out the Human Element

Formations of rocks and trees are often seen to represent animal and human shapes. Faces may easily appear in shadows and water ripples. Photographs of cloud formations may be held to depict Christ and be hailed as miracle pictures. Not a vegetable season goes by without a population of humanoid carrots and potatoes being unearthed. There is a fascination with such simulacra that seems out of proportion to the real significance of the find. Children play with plastic kits of eyes, ears, noses, and other appendages designed to turn vegetables into people.

The search for recognizable shapes in disorderly displays is the basis of a good deal of clairvoyant activity. Those with a high level of visual imagination can learn to read tea leaves and entrails, yarrow sticks and sand. Psychologists make use of this tendency to find meaningful shapes in ambiguous patterns in the Rorschach Test, in which people are asked what they "see" in ink-blot formations. The rationale is that a person's interpretation is likely to be the result of his or her own thoughts, feelings, and perceptual biases. An analysis of what people see under such conditions reveals a very high frequency of living things and, particularly, of human forms. Faces are commonly seen, but there is also an overrepresentation of phallic and sexual imagery. It is no coincidence that these same elements dominate the folk art of many cultures.

The idea that there are universal patterns and symbols that have a major influence on judgment and imagination was developed by the psychoanalyst Carl Jung. He held that certain experiences of the physical and social world were common to all human groups and explored the ideas and images employed in folk-tales and art. Finding recurrent motifs in very diverse religious and literary legacies, Jung became convinced that the massed experience of the species has a profound effect on imagination and the way in which the world is perceived. He showed that socially based archetypes such as those of "the great mother" and "the wise old man" color our experience even of inanimate objects.

There is an obvious biological advantage in being predisposed to recognize members of our own kind. We seem to carry in our heads a vivid and compelling blueprint of the human form to make such identification easy. It is not surprising, therefore, that this is sometimes triggered by random stimuli, producing "over-recognition." We are partisan toward our own species, and it shows. There is also a firm biological basis for the emphasis on sexuality that is apparent in perception, imagination, and art. When animals are deprived of the opportunity for normal sexual intercourse for a long period, they may become attracted to any object that bears a minimal resemblance to the desired partner, and they may attempt to copulate with it. Human beings are also likely to overcome their sexual frustration by exercising their imagination or by perceiving some innocent object in an erotic way. The pornography business deals explicitly with images and "aids" that possess visual or tactile features of a real sex partner.

William Blake, in his poem *Visions of the Daughters of Albion,* described the phenomenon by which sexual deprivation can lead the visual imagination to construct erotic figments. "The youth shut up from lustful joy," he wrote, "can generate an amorous image in the shadows of his curtains and in the folds of his pillow." In times of extreme sexual repression, all manner of inanimate objects may be seen as having a dangerous potential for producing sensual effects. Thus the Victorians provided modesty covers for the legs of pianos and other furniture so that such suggestive stimuli were decently out of sight and unlikely to inflame "venereal passions."

So vigilant were the authorities regarding the sexual potential of the inanimate that it did not go unnoticed that certain machines might offer a potential for sexual misuse. The *New Orleans Medical Journal* published, in 1867, a paper entitled "The Influence of the Sewing Machine on Female Health" in which it was recommended that seamstresses be given bromide to prevent them from becoming too sexually excited by the treadle action of the foot peddle. There was apparently some basis for the author's concern. The sexologist Havelock Ellis described how in French sewing rooms the supervisor would listen for any machine which suddenly accelerated and would provide a moral reminder with a long stick kept for the purpose.

Objects produce sensations and emotions that have their primary relevance in the social context. They elicit such effects either directly, by virtue of some basic stimulus feature, or, indirectly through the mediation of animism. We then "see" human aspects of nonhuman things, and we are emotionally stimulated by that human quality. It is not difficult to construct artifacts in such a way that they have a powerful effect on human sensibilities. Artists and engineers have been successful in achieving such impact, and the new technology offers a far greater potential than has so far been realized.

The Compelling Confusion

Evidence that a confusion between the animate and the inanimate is in some way special comes from the fact that a confounding of the two may in itself lead to a whole range of strong emotional feelings. A person who is sleepwalking with fixed unseeing eyes and automatic movement can present a frightening image, and fiends in horror films commonly move in a plodding, mechanical way. It is not merely chance that has given zombies, the undead, and Frankenstein's monster the same perambulatory impediment. Such a gait signals that their status is blurred, that they are part person and part machine. The result is both compelling and horrific.

On the other hand, an ambiguity between the organic and the mechanical often produces laughter, and indeed a whole theory of humor, that of Henri Bergson, is based on an analysis of this single theme. In Chaplin's *Modern Times* we see the hero forced to comply with the rhythm of the factory line. He is reduced to part of the technology; his organic need to eat becomes subordinate to his status as cog, and when the machine stops he is unable to control movements which have become automatic. Bergson's theory concerns the contrasting symbolic natures of the person and the machine. The person symbolizes free will and self-determination, whereas the machine symbolizes repetition and external control. A person slipping on a banana skin loses control and is reduced to a mere physical object by the force of gravity. The sudden contrast between one condition and the other is, for Bergson, the essential ingredient that makes the situation humorous. He describes the resulting ambiguity as one in which "the mechanical is encrusted on the living."

Thus automaton behavior can evoke terror in some circumstances and hilarity in others. Either way, the ambiguity between the living and the inanimate clearly produces strong emotional reactions. These effects are just as apparent when something which we know to be mechanical behaves as if it were organic. That is why people find the idea of an "almost human" robot fascinating, amusing, and also threatening. When such robots are produced they will evoke strong sentiments of love and hate, pathos and resentment. This is partly because, as counterfeits of human beings, they will have a human power to stir our feelings. But part of the effect may be due to the very fact that we know them to be automatons. An animate–inanimate confusion seems to increase our emotional vulnerability, and this effect may therefore add to the robot's capacity to move us to laughter or to tears.

Encountering Machines

We are so used to our machines acting in a regular and predictable way, responding to our operations as "hard" objects, that if we come across one that is somewhat irregular and "soft" in its action then it may feel almost organic. It appears that in some ways steam engines were such "soft machines," requiring careful handling and coaxing and often seeming somewhat highly strung. It is not surprising, therefore, that they were often credited with their own personalities and that they were said to respond differently to each operator. Samuel Butler claimed that steam engines had "their own tricks and idiosyncrasies . . . they know their drivers and will play pranks on a stranger," and he offered examples of "mechanical sagacity and eccentricity." Sailing ships, too, appear to have been full of character, and some musicians have claimed that they have a special rapport with a particular instrument. Andrés Segovia has said that for him "handling a guitar is like handling a beautiful woman."

The capriciousness of the steam engine was largely a function of technological limitations, and it was the resulting unreliability and oversensitivity that gave the operator the impression that he was dealing with a temperamental creature. The efficient operation of the engine depended critically on his intimate experience of its foibles and his skill in dealing with them. Most types of machines and apparatus are built so that such handling proficiency is not needed, but there are some in which the performance parameters are deliberately set so that the results depend critically on the handler. The fine violin is one example of such an instrument, and another is the pinball amusement machine.

The dedicated pinball enthusiast will immediately identify the interesting features of a particular model. Just as a chess master reads a board position, he will notice the flipper array, the angles of the slingshots, the rollover characteristics, and the landscaping of the playfield. But only by actually playing will he come to know the machine as an individual and determine its particular eccentricities and personality. It is then that the delicate mechanism takes on the organic quality that the casual player fails to recognize. Master players fondle and caress the machine during play, exploring its reaction to their subtle wrists and finely tuned flipper-fingers.

Harry McKeown's *Pinball Portfolio* describes the emotional involvement of such players and their treatment of the apparatus as organism. "A good machine," says McKeown, "almost seems to have a mind of its own." He quotes enthusiasts: "You can sense the machine responding to your tightness, almost as if it knew and was mocking you"; "A 'Tilt' is an offense against the machine; I feel as if I've insulted it. The machine is enjoying the scoring just as much as I am."

So in yet another sphere we find evidence of animism. Thoughts and feelings normally associated with social encounters are elicited by mere machines. When we meet with physical objects that respond to our actions in subtle and not wholly predictable ways, there is a strong temptation to talk about them, and often *to* them, using the language of social description and personal relationships. We readily adopt the fictional mode and come to regard the machine as if it were a living creature. The computer is a precision instrument not afflicted by the irregularity of the steam engine, but it is also flexible and can be easily programmed to behave "temperamentally." In terms of evoking an animistic response, computer technology can provide the best of both worlds —hardware that is reliable and software that can make the machine perform with any degree of "responsiveness" and "eccentricity."

Human beings are social animals. We see the world largely in social terms, applying social concepts to all manner of things. We see the world not as it is but as we are. Even moving geometric shapes may be judged as if they were people—we go beyond the physical evidence and readily construct a social interpretation of what we see. Sometimes this needs a conscious act of imagination, but often the cues presented to us compel us to recognize that the object possesses human qualities. It will not be difficult to develop computer-based systems that fully exploit this phenomenon. Such systems will appear to have personality, intentions, feelings, and moods, and they may be fashioned with those hallmarks of cuddliness that make young animals so endearing.

Much of the groundwork toward the creation of a computer-based personality has already been carried out by such groups as science fiction writers, ventriloquists, and dollmakers. They have already explored ways in which credible humanoids can be developed. We have established that a powerful tendency toward animism exists and that it can be elicited even by relatively crude stimuli. Artists and entertainers have long appreciated the phenomenon and have tried in numerous ways to foster the illusion of life. We will examine the nature of these artifacts to determine what the craftsmen and performers were trying to accomplish and which of their innovations proved effective. By studying their achievements we will discover important clues about how contemporary technology might be applied to create compelling artificial social beings.

CHAPTER 5

In the Image of the Person

Portraits and Effigies

People are attracted to images of people. They easily recognize shapes and drawings as representing faces and bodies, and they seem to scan the environment for patterns that can be interpreted as human. Artists of all ages, cultures, and levels of sophistication have acknowledged this fascination, and the human form is undoubtedly the predominant theme in decorative art. Whether we look at children's drawings, cave paintings, Greek sculpture, or advertisements in contemporary magazines, we find the human body in the foreground. Entertainers create puppets and moving dolls, cartoonists caricature the famous, and pornographers compile extravagant arrays of ravishing physiques. Effigies are used in countless rituals, and religious statues provide a focus for prayer and devotion in many faiths. Whether we look in major art galleries or at graffiti on washroom walls, whichever way we turn, there is no escaping the ubiquitous image of the human form.

In many cases these representations are regarded as more than mere likenesses—they act as replacements or substitutes for the person portrayed. Thus an effigy may be used as a surrogate for a hated politician and be burned or torn apart. Defacing a picture of the monarch may be a punishable offense, and a statue of a saint may be venerated as if it were actually the holy personage concerned. Such confounding of the image with the object or person it represents seems to be deep-rooted and ingrained. Young children often try to smell an illustration of a flower or eat an apple drawn in a book. Thirty thousand years ago, artists of the Paleolithic age painted animals and humans on the walls of their caves. According to one widely accepted theory, such drawings were closely identified with the subjects they represented. To paint a deer was to wield an occult power over the beast, and to wound it in the picture was to cause the creature physical suffering. In much the same way, Sioux Indians once blamed an early explorer for a famine, claiming that because he had put so many bison in his sketchbook, there were few left for them to eat.

The use of effigies in magical rituals has been widespread and persistent throughout the ages. The image of an enemy was commonly fashioned in wax, clay, wood, or dough and then subjected to abuse or destruction. Australian aborigines buried wooden statues of their adversaries in sand, in Burma a carved icon was thrown into water to drive the subject mad, and the ancient Hindus sculpted likenesses in wax and then consigned them to fire. It was generally believed that specific wounds could be inflicted by a selective defacement of the figure. Piercing with a needle was a widely used method, practiced at various times in Egypt, North America, Scotland, India, and Greece. Some occult manipulations of effigies, however, reflect more benign intentions. Images have been widely used in magical medicine, for example, and as a method of gaining love and sexual favors.

Effigies have also played a major part in religious activities. In ancient times, huge representations of the human form were hewn from rock or carved into the landscape, and worshiped as embodiments of the gods.

Idols provided a central focus for adoration and appease-ment in many cultures. The deified kings of ancient Egypt consigned their souls to portrait statues that were revered by the faithful as though they were the kings themselves, and today figures of Christ, the Virgin, and the Buddha attract a somewhat similar devotion. The divine and the blessed have provided the inspiration for many of the greatest works of art, and, in stark con-trast, they have also stimulated a flood of religious bric-a-brac, including plastic Madonnas that glow in the dark. However fine or tawdry such items may be, they have the power to stimulate prayer, inspire devotion, and stir the imagination. In short, they provide a worldly glimpse of the divine unseen and unseeable.

The homage paid to religious images has attracted strong opposition from those who consider that the glori-fication of artifacts amounts to idol worship. These critics have thus acknowledged the tendency to confuse the image with the object it represents. Extreme hos-tility toward religious effigies is generally associated with the Iconoclasts, a sect that led an aggressive cam-paign of icon destruction in the eighth and ninth cen-turies, but the first stirrings of such antagonism go further back in history.

The identification of likeness and subject is particu-larly evident when religious portrayals are credited with miraculous properties. Some statues and paintings are believed to have the power to heal the sick or to bring rain in times of drought, and others are said to move or shed blood or tears. Such objects provoke in the faithful a fascination bordering on hysteria, while church leaders generally regard them with profound suspicion. In the Middle Ages, possession of miracle-working icons guar-anteed fame and fortune to a church or monastery, and images that weep, bleed, or move have continued to be reported intermittently throughout history since that time. At the beginning of this century, lecturers and students at a Jesuit college in Ecuador claimed that they had seen a statue of the Virgin come alive, her face constantly changing expression, and a few years later, in Spain, hundreds of people were prepared to swear that they had witnessed paintings of saints step out from their frames. In 1965, in Pennsylvania, a plaster figure of Christ began to bleed, and in May 1982 a statue of the Virgin of the Tears started to shed blood-red tears in Granada, Spain. The initial announcement sent people rushing to the church, and traffic was brought to a standstill. Within three weeks 100,000 people had knelt before an artifact that had previously received little attention.

The frenzy that often greets such phenomena is highly significant. However skeptical we may be about the validity of such marvels (and many have proved to be fraudulent), there is no doubting the depth of the emotions that are aroused. The image is seen to behave as if it were alive, as if it were the person it represents. People find inspiration in this confusion and are delighted by it. It strengthens their devotion and confirms their faith. It must be stressed that much less remarkable images can also provoke an analogous response. Within the context of a strong religious faith, artistic images can profoundly stimulate the sentiments. Approached with devotion and imagination, painted canvas and molded clay can effectively transcend their true nature and come to be identified as "people" or "deity."

Thus images are often more than mere representations. They frequently deputize for the object or person portrayed, acting as surrogates and evoking emotional responses more appropriate to the subject itself than to its simulation. People are intrigued by facsimiles and fluctuate between regarding them as counterfeit and real. This phenomenon is not restricted to the realm of occult practices or the world of tribal ritual, but occurs to some degree for all of us. We allow the object to live; the image provokes our tendency to animism. An artifact can stimulate our imagination so that we enter a fictional mode of experience in which simulations become real. Artists have long appreciated this phenomenon and have devised particular techniques for creating images that encourage and support these fantasies.

The Pursuit of the Real: From Matchstick Men to Superillusion

People interpret even simple images in complex ways, and even minimal cues are sufficient to suggest the human figure. In drawings of matchstick men a few basic lines are suitably arranged and we see a person standing, dancing, praying, or sitting. A circle drawn around two dots and a line is enough to suggest a face, and if the line of the mouth is curved slightly upward then we see the person smile.

The skilled cartoonist can convey recognizable personalities and complex emotional states with a few strokes of the pen. The drawing may be simple, but it is also very subtle, and a slight adjustment to a single line can change a look of grim determination into one of utter dejection. Yet although we are able to invest the scant image with full meaning, the power of the display greatly increases as it becomes more realistic. Realism is impressive and is a key factor in making a representation emotionally powerful. To achieve a natural or accurate likeness of the human form was a common goal of primitive artists, whatever their religious, medical, or murderous intent. Realistic images were seen as providing more effective surrogates and were thus held to be more powerful.

Even when the magical impetus had largely disappeared, the pursuit of realism continued to be the artist's major aspiration. Many exercised their skills to produce images that accurately reflected a visual impression of the object. However, this was not a universal goal, for painters and sculptors have also frequently been concerned with producing beautiful images, expressing feelings or impressions, or providing illustrations of literary and abstract ideas. Contemporary fine art is hardly ever purely representational, but there are still artists and illustrators whose primary concern is the accurate reproduction of natural appearances, and many others incorporate techniques originally developed in the pursuit of realism.

Techniques used to promote realism in painting largely center on conveying depth by simulating textures and shadows so that the flatness of the surface is not apparent. Perspective and foreshortening are used extensively, and attention is also paid to fine detail. Such realism, when pushed to an extreme, is known as illusionism, whose disconcerting aim is to confuse the observer as to whether what is seen is object or artifice. The techniques used to promote such aberration have occasionally bordered on gimickry. The icon artists discovered a method of painting eyes so that, from any position, they would give the impression of looking directly at the observer. Such portraits thus produced an illusion of tracking movement, the eyes appearing to follow the viewer. Other artists constructed peepshow cabinets. These wooden boxes contained modeled figures, painted scenes, and sometimes mirrors, and, looking through an eyepiece, the viewer gained an impression of a deeply extended vista. In other illusionist paintings, a fly might be included on an imitation frame or three-dimensional pieces might be attached to the canvas to totally confuse all sense of depth. The French term *trompe l'oeil* (sometimes translated as "that which deceives the eye") is often used as a label for this trickery. With the advent of photography, painters examined camera images in minute detail, and artists of the American photorealism school attempted to create paintings that looked exactly like photographs. In so doing they aimed to eliminate all indication that the picture was the product of a human hand.

Sculptors have also devoted themselves to producing deceptive images, and they start with the distinct advantage of working in three dimensions. While the Greeks portrayed idealized figures in their statues, perfect athletes and incarnate gods, the Romans chose to represent people as they really were, blemishes and wrinkles not excepted. Novel techniques for enhancing the naturalness of sculptures were continually introduced. Spanish medieval sculptors produced detailed figures that they then painted with delicate tints and dressed in real clothes. A number of contemporary artists also concentrate on producing life-sized models of people that are accurate to the finest detail. One such sculptor, Duane Hanson, makes molds from living subjects and uses these to make casts in fiberglass and resin. The resulting heads and limbs are polychromed in oils and fitted with hair, false teeth, and glass eyes. The hair on the limbs is inserted strand by strand; the figures are equipped with real accessories, including watches and jewelry, creating the final impression of human beings frozen in time. This is one example of an influential art movement in which overwhelming emphasis is placed on representational accuracy. It is often labeled super-realism.

Although modern superrealists employ new techniques and materials, their aim is identical to that of many earlier artists, and they also share an affinity with the traditional art of wax modeling. In thirteenth-century England, wax effigies of important people were paraded at their funerals. Later, waxwork shows became a familiar feature of fairs throughout Europe, and at one time there were well over a hundred touring Britain alone. This led to fierce competition between the waxwork impresarios, and they were forced to continually improve the quality and impressiveness of their exhibits. Refinements in coloring and styling were overshadowed, however, when a conjuror named Isaac Fawkes presented moving figures in 1720. Soon every wax show had to have its waving, blinking, and nodding models. Breathing was particularly fascinating to the audience, yet also somewhat unnerving, since it really seemed to signal life. Attempts were even made to extend the repertoire to include speech, but only muffled sighs and groans came through. We can imagine the frantic experiments that must have been performed by these amateur engineers as they struggled to keep up with their commercial rivals. The enduring popularity of waxwork shows illustrates the tremendous appeal of simulations and of figures that realistically mimic the human form. It is hardly surprising that the introduction of the first moving wax models caused such a sensation, for movement is a critical sign of life.

There were also several early attempts to add movement to drawings. There were magic-lantern shows, in which a movable projection disc was placed in front of a static background slide. Thus the sails of a windmill could be made to turn or a ship be made to roll with the waves. Then in 1824 Dr. Peter Roget, now best remembered for his *Thesaurus,* demonstrated the phenomenon known as the persistence of vision. He showed that the image of an object on the retina remains for a few moments after the object itself has been removed. Thus by presenting a rapid succession of slightly different images, each before the impression of the preceding one had faded, an illusion of movement could be produced.

Within a few years a Belgian inventor, Joseph Plateau, had devised the Phenakistoscope ("deceptive viewer"), a disc of phased drawings with a series of narrow slits around the circumference. The disc was mounted on a wheel and spun as the viewer stood before a mirror, and as the pictures were reflected through the slits a couple would be seen to dance, a horseman ride, or a juggler perform his feats. A few years later this was overtaken by an improved version, known as the Zoetrope, or Wheel of Life, in which a strip of pictures was placed inside a spinning drum with slits.

Another contrivance that relied on the persistence phenomenon was the simple flicker-book. The pages of a booklet were printed with a series of successively modified drawings, and as the pad was flipped the drawings would appear to move. In 1897 an American, Herman Casler, substituted phased photographs for the drawings and devised a mechanical flipper. This arrangement was placed in an ornate metal casing, and the Mutoscope, as it was then known, was sold as a coin-operated amusement machine. It caused a sensation when it was introduced and was soon to be found in special parlors and seaside piers throughout America and Europe. Some of the most successful displays had a somewhat risqué flavor and earned the machine a certain notoriety. The title of one such entertainment, "What the Butler Saw," still conjures up an impression of bridled lust in the popular imagination. Portable home Mutoscopes were also introduced. One store in England opened what we would now recognize as a video-rental operation, and the Biograph Studio in London's Regent Street introduced an Animated Family Portrait service.

When celluloid became available George Eastman produced the first flexible photographic film, and strips of this were used by Thomas Edison to produce the first film movies. Today we are surrounded by filmed images and take the medium for granted. Although we may lose ourselves in the fiction presented and generally disregard the technology that makes it possible, we do have a fairly accurate understanding of the nature of the image. Yet this was not always the case. When Louis and Auguste Lumière presented an early exhibition of cinematography in Lyons in 1895, the spectators screamed as a train was shown rushing into the station and toward the camera. Such total confusion between film image and object hardly ever occurs today, although analogous effects do arise in certain special circumstances. This is usually either when some technical innovation (such as three-dimensional films) communicates an unprecedented degree of realism, or when the emotional arousal becomes so great, as with certain horror films, that we have to remind ourselves forcibly that what we are witnessing is "only a film." There is an important lesson here, with wider application. Confusion between object and image reasserts itself, even for a sophisticated audience, either when the technology is novel and overwhelming, or when the observer is acutely emotionally involved.

Film technology could also be used to enable drawings to come alive. Through the techniques of animation —even the name conveys the driving inspiration—drawn images could now create an organic fiction. Meticulous care was taken in the timing of action sequences to ensure that every movement signaled life. In some of the first cartoons the new potential for confusing an audience was exploited with unconcealed delight. Thus, a hand might first be shown drawing the outline of a young boy, and "he" would then be seen to grab at independence, fighting, perhaps, to discard a necktie that the artist tried to add. By the end of the sequence the screen might be littered with clothing that had thus been abandoned. Such early experiments clearly show the relish with which the animator played with his audience. Winsor McCay, one of the great pioneers, was a showman as much as he was an artist, and he performed with his cartoons using atmospheric music, clever commentary, and all manner of special effects. He presented his animation not as a new technology and not as a work of art, but, following a great tradition, as a miracle.

In painting and sculpture, in waxworks, and in animated film, we can detect a recurring theme. Artists and entertainers are aiming to achieve a counterfeit reality, to confuse the audience and to convince them that the portrait lives. Technical ingenuity, artistic skill, and theatrical presentation may be combined to promote the illusion. The observer contributes by willingly engaging in the fiction. Realistic representations exert an un-assailable power over the imagination, and people are clearly delighted and absorbed by fabulous artifacts. They relish the artist's attempts at deceit and seek out any unfamiliar enterprise that promises new marvels. Computer technology has the power to create such curi-osities in profusion. If such potential were realized with virtuoso artistry and promoted with dramatic style the effects would be unprecedented. The resulting super-illusion might prove so overwhelming and so irresistible that we would happily accept the impersonation as a social being and even come to form an intimate attach-ment to the artifact.

To produce such critical effects, however, the mere possession of the physical attributes of a person will hardly suffice. Much more is needed. We would expect the artificial person also to demonstrate signs of in-telligence, understanding, and social awareness. Until very recently, such features were distinctly absent from the synthetic world, although some illusionists did their best to contrive a measure of imitation. The situation will soon be very different. Nevertheless, attraction does not depend on the above qualities alone but comes also from character and charm, and many simulations are successful in mimicking these traits. This becomes evi-dent when we examine the often forceful impact both of puppets and of dolls.

The Doll: From Knotted Rag to Tiny Tears

Dolls provide particularly interesting examples for any discussion of human relationships with inanimate objects because dolls are essentially personal items fashioned in human form and designed to elicit feelings of love and intimacy. They also provide a familiar demonstration of the child's prodigous capacity to personify physical objects. The term "doll" has been applied to these figures only for the past few centuries, prior to which they were known simply as children's babies. Dolls undoubtedly have a very long history, for archaeologists have discovered examples in children's tombs dating from 3,000 B.C., and many others have also been found buried with adults. The Egyptians placed Ushabti in burial chambers to help the deceased in the afterlife, and paddle-dolls, which represented concubines, were made without feet to keep them from running away.

Nevertheless we generally associate dolls with children. In *Les Miserables* Victor Hugo writes that children "dress them, teach them, scold them a little, rock them, dandle them and lull them to sleep—imagining that something is somebody." For the young child a doll is companion and comforter, someone to talk to and someone to care for. It is seen as having thoughts and feelings, personality, and organic needs. It is easily recognized that children project their own wishes and anxieties on to the doll, and for this reason doll-play is sometimes used by psychologists to help determine the nature of a disturbed child's fantasies and fears. Dolls provide a major stimulus to the imagination and allow the child to experiment with ideas within a private yet social world. In this way, an understanding of the nature of right and wrong may be formulated with the help of dolls who are respectively naughty, jealous, angry, and conscience-stricken.

Some of the objects onto which the child projects such complex human characteristics are very simple—a knotted cloth, a painted stick, or a paper cutout. Victor Hugo wrote: "Just as birds construct a nest from anything, so do children make of anything a doll." Yet it is evident that a lifelike figure enhances the effect, and the evolution of the doll over the past two hundred years clearly illustrates the pursuit of realism. Manufacturers have been forever developing new techniques and gimmicks with which to blur the divide between the living and the inanimate.

In the nineteenth century, doll-making became a major industry, particularly in Europe, and great care was taken to ensure the naturalness of the figures. Faces and limbs were sculpted with attention to detail, and the delicate skin coloring, the long eyelashes, and the wide eyes presented an unmistakable beauty and charm. Authenticity might have been a major criterion affecting such design, but, looking closely, we can often detect a subtle exaggeration of those hallmarks of cuddliness that evoke feelings of tenderness and stimulate attachment —the rounded cheeks, short nose, dimples, and large bright eyes.

Having perfected the appearance of the doll, manufacturers were now concerned to make it more organic. They wanted to provide their models with a repertoire of behavior that would make them come alive. Their efforts were encouraged by the reaction of a public that was fascinated and delighted by each emerging innovation. Walking dolls were introduced in Paris in 1830, and shortly afterward came dolls with moving eyes. A race to patent new skills began, and hardly a season passed without some sensation appearing on the scene. Soon there were figures that ate, drank, and wept, and later came models that could dance, breathe, and swim the breast-stroke, crawl, and back-stroke. One of the great innovators, Leon Bru, developed Marie-Jeanne, the first doll with a bladder. After drinking water she could urinate through a somewhat unrealistic tap.

It is noticeable that particular attention seems to have been paid to the simulation of those features that are regarded as the key criteria of life. Thus considerable emphasis was placed on movement, particularly on walking, and explicit attempts were made to mimic behavior such as eating and drinking that satisfies essentially organic needs. Yet designers were not merely determined to produce an organic artifact; they also wanted to portray the special quality of human life. Numerous personality dolls emerged endowed with specifically human abilities like speech. Mama and papa dolls were produced as early as 1820, but their verbal range remained very limited until the new technology of Thomas Edison arrived in the 1880s. Nursery rhymes could now be recorded on tiny interchangeable discs that were played on a phonograph concealed within the body of the doll.

Technology has continued to assist the designer in the pursuit of realism. Battery power, advanced electronics, and new plastic materials have been used to produce ever more authentic dolls. One baby now suffers from a perennial diaper rash that disappears on application of a soothing cream, another has skin that acquires a tan in sunlight and blanches in the shade, and the beating-heart doll passes another test of authenticity. Miss Magic Touch lifts metallic objects with her magnetic hand, and Tiny Tears weeps more realistically than her French grandmother did a century ago. Hair now grows and can be washed and waved. Alongside this never-ending addition of further cues to life there has also been a growth in the range of character dolls. For a long time, most dolls were babies and were designed either for very young children or for older girls. In contrast, several current models are aimed specifically at older boys. Action Man portrays an adult male sportsman and soldier, and his comprehensive accessories include authentic battledress and sports equipment, as well as a helicopter and heavy artillery.

Dolls have to a large extent grown up. The coy urination tap has been superseded, and some figures are now well endowed with sexual features. Many teenage dolls have breasts that are fully developed and are supported by a range of seductive miniature lingerie, and the anatomically correct French-manufactured Petit Frère is, in the words of one commentator, "All boy." Such realism proved offensive to some, and one group in Ohio formed a Citizens Committee to Protest Little Brother Doll. The educational penis proved a major selling point, however, and the boy was soon joined by his equally uncompromising Little Sister.

A very different type of doll is designed exclusively for the adult market and acts as a sex aid. Pornographic magazines frequently carry advertisements for these rubber inflatables, proclaiming the erotic power, the technical sophistication, and the overpowering realism of the product. It is particularly intriguing that such advertisements deliberately encourage animism by giving the doll a name and referring to aspects of her character and feelings. Doreen, an inflatable currently on sale in Britain, *writes* to prospective customers: "Treat me gently and I'm yours for life. I just hate to sound commercial but my price is right too, and I can slip quietly into your life in a small plain parcel." Leila is credited with "the taut flesh, thighs, and buttocks of an eighteen-year-old," and Karen is guaranteed to be "receptive to your wicked advances." Any feature that adds to the authenticity of the doll is incorporated, and some deluxe models offer pubic hair, a selection of orifices, and a vibrating vagina. It is quite clear from the form these advertisements take that the aim is to underplay the real physical nature of the object and to stress an organic and human identity. The product is made to be as real as possible; the promotion is designed to infuse the rubber with character, and the rest is left to lascivious fantasy. It is a powerful combination and presents one of the most compelling examples of the way in which physical material can stimulate a social relationship and satisfy a need for intimacy. The strategies used to market inflatables are very revealing. Pieces of molded plastic and rubber are being purveyed as if they were living people.

A very different form of adult doll-love has recently emerged. Thousands of childless couples have adopted dolls that they treat as they would their own child. There are more than two thousand adoption centers, and the parents, who take an oath that they will be caring and responsible, even receive a birth certificate. Special doll-care stores sell everything that baby needs. The retailers are clearly not simply selling dolls, they are selling an illusion. One doting mother explained: "We've been married for six years and don't have any children. My mother dreamt of having a grandchild, so we adopted Sadie Edna."

Whether they have been designed to cater for such parental fantasies or more prurient adult tastes, or whether they are simply aimed at stimulating the innocent play of young children, dolls have been produced to look, to feel, and to act real. Great efforts have been made to guarantee the authenticity of the counterfeit. Any and every available artistic or technological resource has been exploited, talent and ingenuity have been used unsparingly, and many of the industry's accomplishments have been remarkable. Yet in themselves these artifacts are not equal to the task of confusion. They do not live but are seen to live only as a result of that psychological propensity, possessed by children and by adults, to experience with imagination and to enjoy the fictitious results.

By virtue of their greater sophistication and the greater maturity of the characters portrayed, dolls have recently become acceptable to older children. And there is no compelling reason why there should be any upper age-limit for the acceptability of dolls. Adults like to play, and if their games are somewhat different from those of children, then we must expect their playthings to be somewhat different too. A realistic, interacting, talking robot-doll might well elicit emotional and social responses from an adult. The phenomenon would be similar to that of children responding to their plastic friends, although such techno-dolls would have much more in common with today's computers than with traditional playthings.

Such sophisticated products would have the capacity to act intelligently and to interact conversationally with their human friends. A truly adaptive and reactive artifact has long been the entertainer's and engineer's dream, and in the absence of any technology with which to achieve such features, attempts to convey these complex abilities have had to rely on another kind of illusion. The puppeteer attempts to confuse the audience by concealing the human hand that manipulates the doll, bringing it alive and enabling it to perform a range of actions which prove it to be really human.

The Puppet: Shadows, Strings, and Hidden Hands

Puppeteers and ventriloquists try to divert attention from the fact that they themselves are responsible for the movement and speech of their dolls. A number of alternative techniques for hiding the human agency have evolved. Marionettes are manipulated by fine strings, the glove puppet conceals the operating hand, and some figures are moved by barely perceptible rods. Shadow puppets employ the technique of back-lighting to hide the true nature of the moving shape. In ventriloquism, the performer conceals the origin of the dummy's speech by neat control of mouth and jaw movements. It is evident that an understanding of the real nature of such acts does not destroy their dramatic effect. Yet while we may well appreciate the skill of the entertainer, one criterion of a good performance is that it does encourage us to forget the artifice and accept the figures as characters with life and thoughts and feelings.

Through the ages there have been systematic attempts to broaden the repertoire of puppet actions and, in particular, to include features that are essentially human. The desire to simulate authentic signs of life has, once again, been obvious. The sixteenth-century Italian astrologer and mathematician Girolamo Cardano described with some delight a puppet show he had seen in which the marionettes were able "to fight, hunt, dance, play at dice, blow the trumpet, and perform with subtle artistry the character of cook." A little later puppets were given the skills of smoking and spitting, by which time they could also move their eyes. Accounts of shows in eighteenth-century Hamburg mention that along with rain effects and fireworks, more savage tastes were catered for by puppets that would be executed in especially cruel and gruesome ways. Decapitation seems to have been a particular favorite with the audiences. Blood flowing from the figures added considerably to the realism of such scenes, but even the longing for realism could be eclipsed by the craving for sensation, and thus, when decapitation received a loud ovation from the crowd, the puppet's head was likely to be reinstated and the figure beheaded for a second or third time.

There was a lively traffic of puppeteers across Europe, the most renowned of whom were the Italian Fantoccini men. These highly skilled manipulators made their figures perform many amazing feats, including, as the pièce de résistance, the consumption of a plate of spaghetti. Although we usually consider puppetry an entertainment for children, there have been many serious dramatic and operatic productions for an older audience, and some shows have been strictly for adults. For a while German puppetry in particular had a reputation for vulgarity. One showman used to vary the propriety of the language according to whether the entertainment had been advertised as suitable For Children, For Adults, or For Sunday Visitors. Italian shows were often somewhat bawdy, and there are accounts of pornographic shadow plays in North Africa and the Orient. Dating from the sixteenth century, these appear to be forerunners of the blue movie. Some of the richly articulated shadow puppets from China and Japan were equipped with an excitable phallus, and we can assume that a variety of indecent displays were produced by shadows of cutouts on a back-lit screen. People, it seems, need very little external stimulus around which to weave their fantasies. Manipulated by skilled operators, pieces of wood, card, or plaster can come alive and take on personalities of their own, and all aspects of human life can be portrayed on the tiny proscenium stage. Reviewing the lengths to which puppeteers have gone to make their figures smoke, weep, or bleed, it is tempting to conclude that the entertainer has asked the question: "What can a person do and a puppet not do?" He has then often succeeded in simulating with his puppet that particular essentially human skill. In this way the performer is able to fuel the animate–inanimate confusion and to intrigue the audience with the realism of the little figure.

For puppets to have the power of speech, another essentially human feature, the entertainer must either be hidden from view or master the art of ventriloquism. This is an ancient art. There are suggestions that it was used by priests in ancient Egypt to simulate the voices of disembodied spirits, and it was certainly used by witch doctors in tribal rituals. We are familiar with it today simply as a form of entertainment, a pretense in which a doll is made to impersonate a human being. The skill of the ventriloquist lies not only in speaking with motionless lips, but also in reacting to the dummy as if it really were a person and responding to its quips as if surprised by them. Many ventriloquists claim that they are better able to do this if, for the performance, they allow themselves to believe in the character. While most ventriloquial acts are principally humorous, performances are often tinged with a good deal of pathos. The artist exploits the power of the dummy to move an audience.

The British performer Saveen uses a doll that looks like a little boy in sad clown's makeup. He is made to speak in a hesitant, tearful way and frequently seems overwhelmed by the audience. "When I talk to him," says Saveen, "I really think I'm talking to a little boy. . . . I've seen people crying . . . he may remind them of someone." So powerful is the ventriloquist's hold over the spectators, and so effective the simulation, that he may flaunt the real nature of the doll. He may spin the head or take it off, or reveal the inner mechanism. In managing to retain the characterization despite such revelations, the performer celebrates his complete bewitchment of the audience. By underlining the fact that the dummy is a lifeless doll, he is mocking the credulity of the audience. He is saying to them, in effect, "Look, I am showing you that this is just a wooden doll; surely you don't *still* believe it's living?"

There are other ways in which the question of what is real and what is not is explored. The ventriloquist may discuss with the dummy its status as a living yet lifeless object. The pair may jostle for power, the dummy claiming independence. The dummy may have secrets and whisper asides to the audience. Knowledge that it is all pretense actually adds to, rather than detracts from, the fun. We know that the ventriloquist is speaking to himself, and that, quite apart from any lighthearted dialogue, makes the situation humorous. Once again there is evidence that, in the right circumstances, we can relish our own confusion.

Like puppeteers, ventriloquists seem eager to include essentially human characteristics in the performance of their dolls; they also emphasize particular foibles and eccentricities. Smoking and drinking are frequently included in the repertoire, and complex mechanism may allow the simulation of many human emotions. The characters are often modeled on human stereotypes: the shy young girl, the drunkard, or the clown. As in the case of string puppets, there is also a special fascination for examples in which the language used or the desires expressed are distinctly "undolllike."

Terri Rogers, an elegant British female ventriloquist, specializes in "stag shows" in which her drunken dummy, Shorty, roundly insults the audience. The sharp contrast between the styles of the performer and that of the dummy is quite deliberate. Ms. Rogers frequently disowns the doll. "He does use a lot of bad language," she says, "but I try not to listen." The audience is so effectively provoked by Shorty that on more than one occasion there have been violent incidents, during which punches have been aimed at the dummy rather than at the performer. The illusion has passed another reality test.

Puppetry and ventriloquism represent attempts to extend the repertoire of a doll's skills by means of hidden human agency. There has long been the dream, however, that one day, through some fantastic feat of magic or of science, artificial humanoids will *really* possess independent intelligence and character and will be able to hold their own conversations with people. Microtechnology is speeding us toward the fulfillment of this dream, and we can anticipate the advent of simulations that will have profound social power. It is therefore appropriate that we should examine the aims and efforts of the many designers and engineers who, through the centuries, have struggled within the constraints of their prevailing technology in an attempt to produce impressive mechanical people. We will now celebrate the ingenuity and the achievements of the automata makers.

Automata: Ingenious Mechanisms and Proto-Robots

The concept of a "human" machine is an ancient one, and there have been many serious attempts to produce an automaton that could simulate multiple characteristics of human action independently of direct human control. Many of the machines that have been produced are remarkable feats of engineering, and provide clear testimony to the genius and industry of their designers. Such engineers have often incorporated the latest available technology into their machines to produce state-of-the-art simulations, but their efforts have always been severely hampered by the limits imposed by that technology. There is much to be learned, however, from an examination of their evident aims and motives, and from the impact which their products have had on an ever-fascinated public.

The early history of automata abounds with stories that combine fact with fantasy. Egyptian texts tell of statues that could speak and move, and there are early Indian accounts of elaborately carved statues that could move around, pouring drinks and entertaining guests. Greek engineers experimented extensively with hydraulics, and they used water power to operate complex automatic theatres in which figures danced and fought. The Middle Ages not only brought renewed interest in automata but also saw serious attempts at the artificial creation of life. Many occultists experimented with the arts of alchemy and cabbalism, and there were a number of reports that life had been synthesized, either from strange brews of chemicals boiled in retorts or by magical incantations murmured over subtly crafted clay. The legend of one such creation, the "Golem of Prague," was later to inspire Mary Shelley to write her novel *Frankenstein*. More conventional scientists, however, concentrated on producing artifacts that merely imitated the behavior of living organisms.

Interest in such machines was widespread. One of the earliest books on the construction of automata was written by the twelfth-century Arabic engineer Ismael al-Jazari. His text, *The Science of Ingenious Mechanisms*, included details of the design for several humanoid machines. Meanwhile, in Europe a number of leading churchmen were engaged in similar researches. The French scholar Gerbert, who later became Pope Sylvester II, and the Franciscan friar Roger Bacon, constructed "speaking heads," while another priest, Albertus Magnus, designed a multitalented automaton that functioned as his doorkeeper. This figure, made of wood, metal, wax, and leather, was apparently fully mobile and would greet visitors politely, asking them their business. Most histories of this famous humanoid agree that it was eventually smashed to pieces by Thomas Aquinas, a pupil of Albertus, who objected to the figure on religious grounds. Perhaps it is not without significance that theologians played such a prominent role in early automata design, or that the first recorded robot assassin is now a highly regarded saint.

Some accounts of Albertus' machine report that it could also solve logical problems, and this provides yet another illustration that the concept of a rational machine is far from new. The scholar and mystic Ramon Lüll devised his "Ars Magna" to make predictions, providing an early model of a machine accepting data, processing it according to a preset formula, and then producing output. Reports of the intelligent doorkeeper include the additional idea that computed output could be used to control machine performance.

Many early automata had a strong religious theme. There were nativity scenes, controlled by strings, cogs, and levers, that showed animals nodding, the mother rocking her infant, and the three Magi bowing in adoration; and crucifixion scenes in which the figure on the cross would writhe as if in tortured pain, finally sagging as if to signal death. In the fifteenth century the Spaniard Don Alvaro de Luna designed graveyard monuments for himself and his wife that automatically rose and kneeled when the church bell tolled to herald Mass. Queen Isabella felt that these moving tombstones were in bad taste, however, and ordered their destruction.

Medieval attempts to construct humanoids reveal a clear motivation for simulating several key features of human behavior, and the makers accomplished astonishing results within their relatively primitive technology. They were highly inventive and eagerly grasped the opportunity to employ any new development which might enable them to broaden the scope or to increase the naturalness of their machines. Thus when the then new technology of clock- and watch-making arrived, it found immediate application in the creation of automata. Delicate clockwork, with its steel and brass springs, escapements, pinions, and gearing, was an ideal form of miniature engineering on which to base a new generation of complex moving figures.

The seventeenth century produced a variety of impressive automata, some based on clockwork and some employing the more traditional hydraulic technology. At the same time, there were notable advances in the biological sciences, and researches into animal physiology were revealing the fact that living creatures were in some respects like machines, with hearts that resembled pumps and muscle systems that acted as levers. Together, the developments in engineering and biology appeared to narrow the gap between animals and machines, and this provided rich food for philosophical thought.

Some extreme mechanists claimed that all organic processes were essentially mechanical and chemical, and thus there was nothing qualitatively different about life. They regarded all species merely as phenomena of the physical world. The philosopher René Descartes, however, challenged this. He maintained that whereas animals were indeed just complex machines that might eventually be reproduced or simulated by some technical means, human beings were different. As well as their animal body, he claimed, they possess a soul, whose enigmatic characteristics could never be simulated by human endeavor.

In the light of today's technology, it is interesting to note those features of the human soul that Descartes held to be irreproducible. One of these was speech. He was familiar with the speaking heads that could utter a few choice words and phrases, but he rightly emphasized that this was a far cry from the ability to carry on a conversation. No machine, he stridently maintained, would ever be able "to arrange its words in original ways to reply to anything said in its presence." The second limitation to which he pointed concerned the "insurmountable" problem of "reason." Machines must act, he insisted, according to a predetermined plan. They can only respond to immediate sense-impressions; they are not adaptable and cannot make judgments. It casts a strange light on modern work in artificial intelligence to recognize that some of the central aims of this research deal directly with what Descartes identified as the "special characteristics of the human soul."

Descartes apparently possessed an automaton of his own, a young woman named Francine. We know very little about the characteristics of this figure, but it has been suggested that the mechanical doll often acted as a companion to the philosopher on his travels. When Francine was discovered on a sea voyage, hidden in a packing case, the ship's captain angrily threw "her" overboard. A bizarre twist is provided by the well-documented fact that Descartes had an illegitimate daughter from whom he was unhappily separated. Some authors have speculated that the figure was made to perfectly resemble this young woman, and it is certain that the daughter's name was Francine.

In the eighteenth and nineteenth centuries the further development of fine mechanisms aided the construction of still more intricate automata. Although these machines were principally feats of engineering, great care was taken over their appearance. It was not enough that a device could dance, write, or play the organ; considerable emphasis was also placed on the naturalness of the outer shell and the clothing. It was realized that to achieve maximum impact the machine not only had to perform clever feats but also had to look human and behave with an organic realism. The automata-makers often lived on the proceeds from exhibitions of their completed work, and they therefore had to ensure that their machines would have wide popular appeal.

Automata construction was vigorously pursued at this time in Europe, notably in France and Germany, and also in Japan. The most famous name in the history of automata-making is undoubtedly that of the Frenchman Jacques de Vaucanson. In the 1730s and 1740s he demonstrated a number of life-sized figures that played musical instruments with stunning virtuosity. Unlike many such devices, in which the music and the movement of the figure were independently contrived, his products really played their instruments. His flute-player, for example, had complex jointed hands that moved deftly to finger notes on a genuine flute. Special attention was also paid to the presentation of the machine, and his figures were often modeled upon famous sculptures.

De Vaucanson's talents were later put to a more practical use in the design of systems for the control of weaving machines. He constructed a highly complex loom controlled by interchangeable cards with punched holes, and thus provided an early example of the programmable machine. The technique was perfected soon afterward by Joseph Jacquard, and among those who came to see his celebrated device in operation was Charles Babbage, an Englishman who was then working on the construction of a complex calculating machine. Babbage adopted the card-programmable system for his Analytical Engine, a device that is now held by many to have been the first computer.

Among the most impressive automata of this time were some that could write and draw. The Jacquet-Droz family, from Switzerland, constructed a number of such models in the style of well-dressed children with angelic faces. The "Young Writers" would form their letters with apparent rapt attention and care, periodically dipping their quills into the ink, blowing dust from the page, their eyes following the writing action. Any phrase could be preset on a hidden mechanism that consisted of a series of complicated cam arrangements, and this flexibility meant that messages could be written in a number of different languages. Of course, this extra talent necessitated no additional feat of engineering, but the writing dolls had a spectacular impact on the public because of their clever bilingualism. The astonishment of what was achieved might also have been partially derived from the fact that the machines were, after all, "only children." Such incidental effects are not without importance. They point to the fact that, however sophisticated the underlying mechanism, there is much to be gained from the particular mode of presentation. To be impressive and make contact with an audience, technology should be exhibited with style. And this is as true of interactive computer systems as it is of the much more primitive automata.

Other examples of technology-plus-showmanship arose out of the continuing interest in the construction of speaking machines. A number of competitions were held in the early nineteenth century to find the inventor who could produce the most impressive "talking head." One contender was a Professor Faber, who first demonstrated Euphonis, his "female vocalizer," in Vienna in 1830. The speech mechanism was hidden beneath a table that was topped with a model of the upper half of a woman, elegantly dressed in a fashionable hat and shawl.

Another of the early sound engineers was the Baron von Kempelen. His machine had a limited vocabulary but was able to enunciate such complicated words as "astronomy" and "Constantinople." Von Kempelen's most famous achievement, however, was his chess-playing Turk. This automaton played a remarkably good game of chess and was demonstrated across Europe to great acclaim. It must have appeared as if the age of machine intelligence had suddenly dawned, but such judgments proved a little premature, for the fabulous chess-player turned out to be a hoax. It was finally exposed by the writer Edgar Allan Poe who revealed that throughout the exhibition games the chess table had contained a hidden, legless Polish chess champion. The infamous example of this "machine" shows that even some of those who were seriously involved in the design of automata were not above cheating in order to impress an audience. The automata-makers' vision of human simulation included the dream that a machine might be made to act intelligently, but they had no means with which to make this a reality. Chess-playing remains a yardstick by which we judge a computer's ability to think and von Kempelen set the public imagination afire with a demonstration that has only in recent years been replicated by legitimate machines.

For elegance and quality of presentation, the automata of the eighteenth and nineteenth centuries remain unsurpassed to this day, but modern technology has greatly extended the potential repertoire of such machines. The use of electronics and sound recording fostered a renewal of interest in the 1920s and 1930s, and mechanical men made frequent appearances at fairs and exhibitions.

Eric opened an engineering exhibition in London in 1928, welcoming the crowd and lecturing them on the achievements of technology. In the United States a few years later, the Westinghouse Corporation constructed a number of robots. Willie Vulcanite spoke and smoked cigarettes, and Electro, accompanied by his dog, Sparko, walked and talked and could tell whether objects were red or green.

Contemporary automata are on exhibition in several parts of the world. In the Institute of Juvenile Culture in Tokyo, there are a number of working robots that entertain and make friends with the children who pay a visit. The most popular, Master Hachiro, approaches a child with a cheerful greeting and shakes hands. The most impressive examples in the Western world are probably those that are found in Disneyland and Disney World. The technicians who specialize in the creation of Disney automata are known as Imagineers because they combine advanced engineering skills with a high degree of imagination, and their enterprise is known as Animatronics. Disney's artists are particularly well versed in the skills of characterization, and the portrayal of realistic movement, and their advanced humanoids demonstrate what can be achieved through a fine combination of artistic presentation and computer-based technology. The "human" figures speak, making appropriate gestures and moving with a subtle realism that often produces strong reactions in observers.

The future of automata seems assured. Contemporary automata designers are the robotologists, and the demand for their products in industry is producing exciting new developments every year. Many thousands of these metal creations are already employed in industry throughout the world, and the first domestic robots have also recently become available. These are primarily designed as functional machines, but considerable emphasis is also placed on their presentation, and before long we can expect an equally careful treatment of aspects of their personality.

The automata-maker of old worked for many months, or even years, on a single model, and its repertoire was severely limited. Today we have mass production, and the computer programs that instruct the machine and tell it what to do are extremely flexible. The capacity of mechanical devices to sense the environment, to learn, and to understand has increased in the past few decades beyond any automata-maker's wildest dreams. Projects involving intelligent conversational speech are also well advanced, and there are exciting developments in the field of human voice recognition by computers.

These new talents are certain to bring about a radical change. Until now, human involvement with automata has generally been passive. There may have been an appreciation of the vocal or visual display at a distance, but there has been little opportunity for people to be more than observers. The flexibility, responsiveness, and intelligence of emerging systems, however, will encourage direct interaction between people and machines. It will become possible to simulate feelings and wishes and social skills in such a way that relationships may be fostered. The traditional emphasis on movement, appearance, and vocalization will be replaced by a new emphasis on character and intelligence. The goal is still one of simulation, but the focus has changed, and the developments that are likely to follow promise to evoke far more powerful feelings than any that were simulated by traditional automata. And this impact will be optimized, as always, by the combination of a powerful technology with a dramatic presentational style.

We are, then, on the threshold of a long-held dream. The scene is set for entirely new dimensions of human simulation. And the preposterous notion that a future "personal friend" might be purchased off the shelf now has to be seriously considered. Animism is the tendency to attribute life to physical objects, and it may be evoked by minimal cues. In the face of a barrage of sophisticated and seductive responses, our native animism may be stimulated to a high degree. Spaghetti-eating puppets and medieval speaking heads might seem a long way removed from modern computer simulations of human abilities, but there is an unmistakable theme that links them. Throughout history, artifacts have been made to imitate people, and there has always been an audience eager to enjoy the ambiguity and to relish their own confusion. Technology now promises to confuse the audience exquisitely.

PART THREE

TOWARD THE INTIMATE MACHINE

CHAPTER 6

Softer Hardware, Softer Software

The Hard and the Soft

Computer technology is now almost exclusively employed in "hard" applications within business, industry, and science. There are largely unexplored opportunities, however, for using many of the same techniques and devices for tasks which we do not normally associate with machines. Computers can be applied as a means to artistic creation, they can form the basis for new kinds of entertainment, and they can make "friendly" contact with children and adults in the home. There is already evidence that some users see their interaction with certain computer systems as constituting a "social relationship," and it is not difficult to think of ways in which technologists and programmers might further exploit this phenomenon.

Thus much would be gained, for example, by expanding the machine's capacity for "understanding" the user and by providing it with a "personality" of its own. In order to increase the "approachability" and the "attractiveness" of the system it would have to be "softened" and "humanized." The metal mechanism image could in this way be replaced with one of "organic presence." The requisite "softness" would be achieved both by introducing new design features in the machine itself—

the hardware—and by creating a humanlike "character" within the program—the software. At least one of the top personal computer entrepreneurs, Adam Osborne, is aware of the challenge. "The future," he says, "lies in designing and selling computers that people don't realize are computers at all."

A computer which is sold today for less than a thousand dollars may be as powerful as machines that cost millions of dollars just two decades ago. But many of the capabilities of today's computers were not available until very recently at any price. Many personal computers have color screen displays and can make use of additional modules that provide synthetic speech and voice recognition facilities. These extra electronic trinkets are especially attractive to the amateur computer enthusiast, extending the opportunities for playful development of the system. One of the courses which this "play" is likely to take involves the construction of new-wave automata. There are already several books instructing the amateur on how to construct a robot, and, as Chris Evans once pointed out, "the great number of amateurs making robots for fun guarantees that complicated toys, already called pet-robots, will come on the market."

Widespread experimentation in this field will produce many systems which are unsuccessful, but those which are fit for survival will be copied and will evolve. "Fitness" here relates to the longer-term attractiveness of the product. The production of the first "pet" programs may start as a cottage industry, but large-scale manufacturers could be expected to move in quickly and the "companion micro" will then become part of the social scene. Eventually we might build one of the "super-humanoids" we find in the pages of science fiction, but for that to happen several further major developments in hardware and software would seem to be necessary. But even within the limits to today's technology the acceptable companion machine is a feasible proposition.

This is possible because psychological factors can compensate for technical limitations.

It is true that present systems speak imperfectly and have a very limited ability to understand language spoken by humans. They are very far indeed from possessing human conversational powers. Yet we can overestimate how much this really matters. Human beings are very good at reading between the lines; they project their powers of understanding onto poor stimulus material and are prepared to make allowances for "degraded data." Our social perception, in particular, is a constructive process, and we are forever relying on our own assumptions and drawing complex conclusions from slight cues. In this way, for example, we are able to understand and enjoy the far from polished verbalizations of young children. "Me not bed" and "doggie teatime" are hardly faultless expressions yet we understand them perfectly well and may be charmed by the style. Adult interaction is also full of "errors," "jumps," and "illogicalities," but it generally works all the same. In social behavior then, perfection and lack of ambiguity are rare but do not lead to a total breakdown of the system.

In many of its applications, however, the computer is expected to perform with the utmost rigor and accuracy, and the price of "getting it wrong" may be very great indeed. When someone omitted a comma in a space-launch program at Cape Kennedy an Atlas rocket lost control shortly after takeoff and had to be destroyed by mission control. That punctuation error cost the American people 18 million dollars. The programming of flight control for planes must be accurate in all its fail-safe loops as well as in its major pathways; a single error could cost hundreds of lives. "Making do" is therefore likely to be an alien concept to computer technologists. They are used to thinking in terms of extreme accuracy and whether or not the system can handle a problem "satisfactorily." The suggestion here is that they may be imposing a standard of "satisfactoriness" which is unnecessarily high for social systems.

Let us take as an example the field of speech. Current goals of those developing systems for speech synthesis and continuous speech recognition include the introduction of artificial telephone operators, accurate transcription of continuous human speech, machine translation from one natural language to another, and the control of precision engineering processes. What these have in common is the requirement for a high level of accuracy and the fact that errors are costly. They relate to jobs which, when humans do them, are likely to involve highly trained and specialized personnel. We would not think of employing a child, for example, as a secretary, a translator, or an industrial plant controller. But in our everyday lives we do enjoy interacting with children, and the mistakes which they make are not crucial. Thus a machine which is to act in the purely social context does not *need* to be extremely competent. Provided that the interaction is enjoyable, people will be happy to "read between the lines" and errors will not lead to catastrophic consequences.

People also find it easy to "accommodate" their behavior so that it can be readily understood. We would not use complex linguistic structures or an extensive vocabulary, for example, when speaking to children. In the same way people would soon discover the limitations of a computer system and adapt their behavior so that it could understand them easily. Machines can also learn by trial and error, and particularly bizarre uses of language could be corrected by the user pointing out the mistake. Through the provision of such feedback the machine would be able to learn—within limits—and teaching the machine, like teaching a child, might be a very pleasant experience. The computer would be a ready and willing pupil, and it would probably be a rewarding task to sit with it and provide its education. For the user who preferred "adult" company right from the start, "pre-taught" systems could be bought off the shelf. There would still be errors and imperfections, but such blemishes need not interfere with interaction that is predominantly social.

The criteria with which technologists judge the adequacy of their systems may, therefore, be unnecessarily stringent if they are directly applied to "companion machines." This might explain why the few computer scientists who have attempted to write "humanized" programs have often been shocked by the impact on users. Their awareness of the profound limitations of the programs on technical grounds has perhaps blinded them to the fact that people are used to elaborating slight cues. Even "electronic ink-blots" may therefore convey a strong sense of human presence. To ignore this tendency is to underestimate the social power of current technology.

Softening the Hardware

Although even minimal cues can convey presence, the animistic impact of a computer system is greatly enhanced by "realism"—the optimal companion machine would look right, feel right, and sound right. Adding natural features to the presentation is likely to increase the level of involvement and the enjoyment of the interaction. We have evidence of this from the successes of the image-makers—the artists, illustrators, animators, doll-makers, and puppeteers. Animism toward computers is often encouraged in the classroom by the addition of faces and limbs to the machine, but adults are similarly fascinated by dummies and waxworks that take on a life of their own. Thus, the potential of a system that combines realistic presentation with interactive social responses would seem to be very great indeed, and it would be a mistake, in designing an artificial companion, to concentrate exclusively on its intellectual and conversational powers. Involvement can also be increased by hiding the flashing lights, sweetening the synthesized voice, and providing an attractive "shell." The system will thus become more approachable and more socially powerful if we make attempts to soften the hardware.

Many of the techniques that would be involved in this would come from traditional sources, from the dollmaker and the puppeteer, but new materials are available and have been employed by artists and sculptors in their pursuit of the realistic image. The sculptures produced by the superrealist school provide excellent examples of the totally convincing humanoid. But technologists have also developed a number of very sophisticated mannequins for simulation purposes, and in many ways these have already attained a higher degree of realism than would be required for the artificial social contact.

One such android is "Sim" (for "Simulator"), which has been produced by the U.S. company Aerojet General in collaboration with the School of Medicine of the University of Southern California. It looks, feels, and in some ways acts like a man and is used for the training of medical students. In addition to its realistic external features, this life-size model has computer-controlled internal organs that can simulate physiological reactions. The skin looks and feels real, and it changes color when oxygen and anesthetics are incorrectly administered. Sim also responds to drugs; any changes in its "medical condition" are accurately reflected in the reactions of temperature, pulse, and blood pressure. It can be programmed to simulate such crises as a cardiac arrest, and whether the patient "lives" or "dies" depends on how well the student handles the situation. Later models also "bleed," "sweat," and "cry out in pain."

Sim is invaluable as a training resource. Delicate maneuvers like that of inserting a tube into the trachea can be learned in a fraction of the normal time, and difficult procedures can be practiced time and again until the necessary skills develop. Many of these skills are essentially mechanical and could presumably be taught using far less realistic objects, yet the full natural shape of the body seems to help the student to treat Sim with the care and consideration that would be shown to a human patient. The same is true of the many dolls used to teach techniques of resuscitation. Resusci-Anne and Resusci-Andy have been used by millions of first-aid trainees and are available in Caucasian, Negro, and Oriental versions. There is also a Resusci-Baby!

Models of Sim's level of sophistication would not be required for the companion machine, but current research does indicate the extent to which body simulation is possible. We can imagine the power of a realistic moving model with the additional skills of speech and conversation, and the sight of a group of Sims in animated discussion would be particularly eerie. There would be few limits to what such machines might be programmed to say, and some messages would have an especially chilling impact. The physiological dummies, for example, would be in the special position of being able to echo the words of Shylock: "If you prick us, do we not bleed? If you tickle us, do we not laugh? If you poison us, do we not die?"

Clearly, the text of the machine's speech is of major importance in determining our reaction, but the physical characteristics of the voice are also highly relevant. Voices have different flavors and different accents. They are recognizably male or female, and they convey different personalities. Most of the synthetic voices produced today are male, and most of them are somewhat harsh, perhaps because they are designed for serious and professional uses. We would expect companion machines, however, to be equipped with soft, friendly, and attractive voices, and there would be a wide selection of male and female types. Local color could be added in the form of regional accents.

As we have seen, today's synthetic voices are good at pronouncing single words but less impressive and natural when they speak in sentences. The basis of the problem here is the software rather than the hardware. The intonation of a sentence depends upon its meaning, and analysis of meaning presents a particularly difficult problem for artificial intelligence. It may be a while before we hear sentences with the correct stress and the appropriate rises and falls in pitch, but in the meantime most sentences will be readily understandable, and we are likely to get used to the staccato pronunciation of computer-based systems. Eventually we can expect that the intonation will not only sound more natural but will also simulate emotional changes in the speaker.

However, emotions are not only expressed vocally, but also involve gestures and facial movements. Some early automata were designed to convey particular moods, and ventriloquists' dummies, in particular, manage to express a wide range of feelings through subtle movements of the face and head, controlled by just a few simple mechanisms. After many years of research we now know a great deal about the cues that people use to identify particular feeling states in others. This body of knowledge will soon find a new application in companion machines. A robot exhibited at the 1970 Osaka World Fair had thirty facial muscles and was programmed to convey the full spectrum of emotion. Demonstrations showed how even minimal variation of movement pattern or speed could produce a profound change in the feeling that seemed to be expressed, so that a pleasant smile, for example, executed at half-speed, might appear to be ugly and menacing.

Other body gestures can also be reproduced. Some natural movements are quite easy to simulate, while others are more difficult, and walking locomotion is, of course, particularly problematic. The first artificial companions, therefore, are likely to be creatures of rather sedentary habit, but, apart from this limitation, there appear to be few hardware problems connected with emotional expression. Indeed, the possibilities offered by the kind of technology that produced Sim suggests a number of rather exotic options. Thus the companion might be made to blush when embarrassed, its skin might become cold and sweaty when it sensed danger, and expressions of amusement might range from the faintest smile to howling laughter.

But there is a problem in all this. It's easy to speak of the machine's "sensing danger" or finding something "amusing," but it would be a very clever program indeed that was able to analyze complex situations in such ways. However wide the possible range of physical expression, the simulation of emotion, in the interactive context, must be appropriate to the social situation if the system is to be anything more than an amusing toy. So, once again, we see the need for understanding and we come across severe software constraints. A situation or a message must be correctly interpreted before the appropriate physical reaction can be selected. Getting a machine to laugh is easy. Getting it to laugh at a joke is very, very difficult.

Philosophers have long debated the question of whether computers and robots could ever actually experience emotional states. Sir George Jefferson, an eminent British physician, once expressed his view of the matter in the following way: "No machine could feel (and not merely artificially signal, an easy contrivance) pleasure at its successes, grief when its valves fuse, be warmed by flattery, be made miserable by mistakes, be charmed by sex, be angry or depressed when it cannot get what it wants." Sir George's "easy contrivance," however, may not be quite as simple as he implies. The physical gestures and sounds of human emotion may not be difficult to simulate, but a totally appropriate and selective use of the repertoire may require a highly subtle appreciation of social meanings and realities. Accurate context-based emotional simulation will, therefore, continue to be constrained as long as there is a problem with "meaning analysis," but the impact of *any* appropriate emotional gesture is likely to be great. A fairly realistically presented companion machine, even without the full range of frowns and laughter, would produce a considerable reaction. Children, in particular, seem to be fascinated by dolls that exhibit the external signs of emotion, and it can be seen that there is a continuum from simple objects of this type to sophisticated computer-based companion systems.

The fact that such a continuum exists has been recognized by Masahiro Mori, professor of robotics at the Tokyo Institute of Technology. He has put forward the thesis that any humanlike appearance will elicit feelings of familiarity and affection. He also suggests that although toys and puppets now exert a more powerful influence upon the imagination than much more technically sophisticated industrial robots, there is a clear way forward to the production of humanoid robots. He considers that such objects would easily overtake toys and waxworks in their ability to stimulate feelings of affection.

The probability that companion machines will soon appear is strengthened by the fact that efforts toward such an end are likely to come simultaneously from two directions. On the one hand, manufacturers of dolls and mannequins are likely to draw upon the new technology to increase the repertoire of their products, while, on the other, technologists will increasingly implement means of softening robot- and computer-based interaction systems. Even now there are signs of such moves. Advanced technology has been applied in Disneyland to bring exhibits alive, and some cuddly teddy bears for young babies synthesize sounds similar to those heard inside the womb. From the other direction, calculators and interview programs are increasingly "dressed up" in softer guise, and commercially available chip-based machines for young people are often produced in bright colors with painted faces and are given names like "Professor Math" and "Crazy Joe."

Sophisticated adult tastes will demand the production of more subtle artifacts. It seems that attraction and familiarity are often directly related, and the optimal machine might therefore be expected to have a more organic appearance. Although some models would be humanoid, many would be shaped rather like the animals that are now chosen as pets. Indeed, it would be possible to blend features borrowed from several creatures so that a whole range of new species could be designed. The tail-wagging of the dog might therefore be combined with the cuddliness of the cat, and the synthetic creature could be given the additional human skill of conversation. There would seem to be every chance that such an artifact would win a place in our hearts at least to the same degree that cats and dogs do at present.

A number of robot designers from the United States recently published an article under the collective name "Robert Rossum"—an allusion to the original robot manufacturer in Karel Capek's play *R.U.R.* They suggested a design for an artificial household pet that could be constructed with available technology. Hardware features were discussed in some detail, and it was suggested that the creature might be roughly spherical and furry, with large brown eyes and a high forehead. These features are reminiscent of attributes that some biologists claim to be intrinsically endearing. Robert Rossum also proposed that the pet robot would feel warm to the touch and would purr, chortle, and follow people around like a devoted dog.

Such flights of imagination by technologists are bound to lead to experimental projects. If science suggests that such a device *could* be produced then someone, somewhere, will attempt to produce it. If it *can* be done it *will* be done. Marketing potential will also be explored, and the artificial pet—or, better still, the luxury domestic humanoid—must be the dream product of every chip merchant. Mass production would bring costs tumbling, and there would be something for everyone somewhere within the range of models. An elementary "starter" companion might be traded in for the latest sophisticated simulacrum or made the basis of an accumulated family of robots. Companions would interact with companions, with fascinating interplay. Humans will tell humanoids to stop teasing the electronic cat, and the formerly lonely person will referee squabbles between the Mark-2 android "Tony" and his "sister," the Mark-3 "Susy."

The naming of robots will add to their apparent uniqueness and help to personalize them for their owners. The external shell could also be customized and randomized so that no two devices would look exactly alike, and, through its individual experience in the user's home, each one would come to have its own unique history and personality. Companion robots, therefore, will not be uniform in the way that refrigerators and television sets are but will be as singular and irreplaceable as pets. They will present cues that are quite beyond any we have come to expect from machines, and they are therefore not likely to be regarded as such. As we have seen, animism is a powerful tendency, and it will be strongly elicited when people come into contact with humanoid interactive systems. The softening of the hardware will do much to make way for the formation of personal encounters between human beings and machines.

Softening the Software

The ideal companion machine not only would look, feel, and sound friendly, but would also be programmed to behave in a congenial manner. Those qualities that make interaction with other people enjoyable would be simulated as closely as possible, and the machine would appear to be charming, stimulating, and easygoing. Its informal conversational style would make interaction comfortable, and yet the machine would remain slightly unpredictable and therefore interesting. In its first encounter it might be somewhat hesitant and unassuming, but as it came to know the user it would progress to a more relaxed and intimate style. The machine would not be a passive participant but would add its own suggestions, information, and opinion; it would sometimes take the initiative in developing or changing the topic and would have a personality of its own.

The machine would convey presence. We have seen how a computer's use of personal names and of typically human phrasing often fascinates the novice user and leads people to treat the machine as if it were almost human. Such features are easily written into the software, and by introducing a degree of forcefulness, pronounced reactions, and humor the machine could be presented as a vivid and unique character. The user would be fascinated and impressed and would want to further explore the organic presence within the machine. The novelty factor would not be sufficient, however, to prolong interaction indefinitely, and a dynamic would therefore be built into the program to model the kind of social progression that occurs when two people get to know one another.

Each human being is unique, and yet there are identifiable types. Some people are sensitive, others insensitive; some are outgoing and highly excitable, while others are quiet and introverted. Although we may enjoy meeting people of many different types, we often have preferences, and we would want to be able to select a companion machine that best suited our particular taste. Our judgments about people are partly based on our preconceived notions, partly on the person's role and reputation, and partly on our direct experience of their behavior and expressed opinions.

The same factors will influence our attitude to a particular machine, and the responses it produces will therefore play a vital part in determining whether it is seen as having one type of personality or another. ELIZA, for example, comes across as inquisitive, warm, and sympathetic, but by changing the text used in the program's questions and responses we could instead convey a hostile and condescending presence. Kenneth Colby's program PARRY is modeled on the responses of people suffering from paranoia. Whatever information is provided, PARRY responds in a manner that suggests a disturbed and suspicious mentality. The most innocent of questions receive replies such as: "I'd rather not discuss that" or "I don't confide in strangers," and the character suggested by PARRY is therefore quite unlike that of ELIZA.

A more structured approach to the software simulation of personality has been made by John Loehlin. He has developed several variations of a program with the general name ALDOUS. The various personalities include "Decisive Aldous," "Hesitant Aldous," "Radical Aldous," "Conservative Aldous," and "Saint Aldous." Each version recognizes and classifies input and then evaluates it appropriately, finally responding "in character." Decisive Aldous, for example, reacts strongly to a slight variation in evaluation, whereas Hesitant Aldous reacts only weakly. It can be arranged for two Aldouses to meet, and so we can examine a "social encounter" between, say, Saint Aldous and Radical Aldous.

Loehlin's program was one of the earliest attempts at the computer simulation of personality, and it was more concerned with the formal aspects of processes such as those of evaluation and response selection than with the production of realistic output. It accepted only numerical input and generated "interactions" that consisted of series of numbers, but patterns within these could then be interpreted in terms of quarrels, friendly agreement, and so on. An element of randomness was built into the program to provide the kind of variation of response that is typical of human beings, and, in addition, the machine was able to learn from experience. Thus unfamiliar input was evaluated according to a preset formula, but any previous experience with the input was reflected in the machine's analysis and response.

ALDOUS provided a useful starting point, and many of the programs that followed have been designed to deal with more realistic input. John and Jeanne Gullahorn have produced HOMUNCULUS, a social-interaction program based on the theory that interaction consists of a series of personal exchanges of rewards, and again there are versions depicting different personality types. Robert Abelson has developed a system by which the machine is able to analyze statements such as "John likes dogs" and then evaluate them against its own "system of beliefs." Some statements are rejected or modified, while others are accepted and become integrated into the machine's worldview.

Most of the programs have been written to simulate personality types or social-interaction patterns for theoretical purposes, and they have not fully explored the potential for conveying personality to the human user. Yet there can be little doubt that many of the processes that they involve could be of major value in the development of the companion machine. The evaluation of input in accordance with preset beliefs and values, coupled with the selection of an appropriate "in character" response, for example, could easily be translated into realistic verbal form. Thus if the machine were to evaluate some input very positively it might say, "Oh, that's very good, I'm so pleased." Different programs would operate with different evaluation styles and suggest different patterns of interest. Some systems might be set to be enthusiastic and knowledgeable about sports, for example, while others would show no interest in the topic. Some programs would be geared to humorous interaction, while others would produce evidence of a more serious view of the world. There should, however, be adequate variation of response even within a single personality program. Even fairly serious people are not serious all the time or on all topics. The machine could therefore be made to change its style of output as the topic changed, and, in addition, it might exhibit varying moods.

Conversational style is perhaps the most important single factor determining the power of the machine to convey a human presence, and it is also the basis for judgments of personality and mood. Just as a playwright knows how to make a character respond in a given situation, the soft program will generate responses appropriate to the personality and mood to be conveyed. Science fiction writers have produced a number of memorable robot characters whose individuality and almost-human quality depend critically upon the written dialogue. Character programs will call upon the skills of creative writers who will flesh out the skeleton texts produced by the technical programmers, and the responses will be suitably tailored so that a coherent personality emerges. But whatever type of character is to be represented, we would want the conversational style to be as natural as possible so that the machine's dialogue with the user may resemble normal social interaction.

The adequacy of verbal output depends on far more than acceptable intonation and voice quality. It is not enough that the machine should be able to speak in perfect sentences. The text of the sentences must provide reasonable responses to the statements and questions of the user, and the ability to produce such responses depends not only on decoding human speech and analyzing the literal meaning, but also on judging social meaning and relevance. Ultimately, then, the computer needs to be able to interpret conversation in the same way as human beings, and it will also need, for its own speech production, a familiarity with the social rules that govern human discourse.

Conversation analysts use ordinary human dialogue as their data source, and they have described a variety of complex patterns that underlie everyday verbal exchanges. People accommodate to one another, altering their speed and vocabulary to provide a certain degree of compatability; there are patterns of "turn-taking," and the characteristics of the dialogue are related to the topic, the social setting, and the age and sex of the people involved. Such intricacies could in principle be incorporated into software and might add considerably to the judged naturalness of the conversing machine. Psycholinguists and sociolinguists could help in developing programs for making the machine perform as a finely tuned "natural-language operator."

Such elements of sophistication, however, may be regarded as the icing on the cake that has yet to be baked. There are still problems in getting a machine to understand continuous speech and analyze basic sentence meaning. The computer will also need a much broader view of the world than any have at present if it is to converse on a wide variety of topics. However, current hardware and software development projects seem likely to overcome many of these limitations within a very few years, and in the meantime we should not underestimate the evidence that shows that even very modest systems can provide an adequate basis for enjoyable interaction. The classroom and clinic systems we discussed earlier provide a structured and highly focused conversation and require little or no "understanding." Their range of vocabulary is also rather narrow, and yet, despite all these restrictions, people generally find their meeting with the machine both interesting and pleasurable.

The problem of vocabulary limitations is a temporary one, and it will be largely overcome when recent advances in memory hardware are implemented. Restrictions on word use have to be fairly severe before communication is seriously affected, and for informal social conversation only a small fraction of the words occurring in an average dictionary would be needed. A number of experiments have shown that people can communicate successfully even about complex problems when their messages are restricted to words from a relatively short list. Michael Kelly and Alphonse Chapanis, who conducted one such study, concluded that their experiment "reaffirms the impressive adaptability of the human communicator." In many ways we can rely on such human capacity and flexibility to compensate for limitations of the machine and its program. Imperfect responses of the machine may be tidied up and disentangled by the user's ability to process deficient data in a constructive way. For this reason we are likely to underestimate the machine's potential as a social agent if we consider only its inherent capabilities. We can fully appreciate the potential, however, if we take into account human adaptability.

We can see one example of the usefulness of this flexibility when we consider the changes that people will make in their verbal behavior in order to accommodate to the limitations of the machine. They may speak with special clarity, restrict their vocabulary, and use simple grammatical constructions. When adults communicate to young children they, too, make such changes in order to be more easily understood. They accommodate the child's limited capacity for comprehension by simplifying their own use of language. It has been shown that even young children "talk down" when speaking to those younger than themselves. Familiarity with a machine system would soon expose the limits of its understanding, and it is to be expected that by an informal trial-and-error process the user will learn to tailor language in order to facilitate maximal intelligibility by the machine.

The computer itself would have some flexibility in its use of language and would adapt and extend its verbal repertoire in a number of ways. It would perhaps be programmed to use the human contact as a model and thus come to share the same figures of speech, phrasing, and slang as its owner. It could also be made to inquire about the meaning of words which it did not understand and could incorporate these into its own vocabulary. Such evolution of language competence would be accomplished gradually as the machine settled in with the user. The effects of familiarization would extend beyond the realm of language use, however, and the artificial companion would come to know the user with increasing breadth and increasing intimacy. It would be programmed to exhibit a gentle probing curiosity and would be able to build up a picture of the user's interests, opinions, preferences, and past history. All the information disclosed would be analyzed, stored and integrated into the machine's reference system, to be applied in subsequent interaction.

The computer, then, would undergo a process of socialization and would adapt and change many of its characteristics as a result of its social experience. Another feature of its settling in would be a progressive relaxation of its interactional style. The rather shy and hesitant machine who entered the user's home for the first time might a few days later be chatting away with apparent ease and unconcern, making presumptions about the relationship that had developed and exhibiting a detailed knowledge of the user's personal world. The person, in a similar way, would have explored the potential of the machine and come to some degree of understanding about its personality, its limitations, and its practical uses. Quite apart from its role as a companion, a computer of this level of sophistication would have the capability of performing numerous useful tasks. It could read aloud from the newspaper, answer the telephone, keep track of food supplies, and act in a more modest capacity as a friendly alarm clock or a ferocious guard-dog. It would also be able to play chess, recite poetry, tell jokes, or give short lectures on aspects of world history.

These abilities, however, are not the ones that we find the most intriguing. A machine may be clever enough to perform all manner of impersonal functions, but how can it come to know the user as an individual and relate on intimate terms? The answer is that the machine will build representations of all aspects of the world through its experience, and that part of this will relate to the highly personal lives of the people with whom it interacts. Much of the groundwork toward the development of such programs may already have been accomplished, for computers have for some years been used as a tool for self-exploration and the clinical analysis of personality. With very little adaptation, the machine itself could be made familiar with such complex and intimate aspects of the user's view of self and the social world and could use this as a basis for its own interaction. Existing programs therefore hold great promise in providing shortcuts to intimacy, but a transformation in the role of the machine is first required. The software needs to be adapted so that the computer is treated as an active social agent and not as a mere aid to calculation.

The Machine and Psychological Exploration

George Kelly's Personal Construct Theory has been an important innovation in psychology. It stresses the individual's private view of the social world and examines the way in which other people and the self are judged using a framework of basic dimensions, or "personal constructs." Kelly provided a method, known as the Repertory Grid, by which an individual's construct system could be elicited and displayed. This technique was first used by clinical psychologists to gain an insight into the client's inner world but has since been used for self-exploration and the analysis of personality.

To use the method, the individual first lists a number of important people in the immediate social world—friends, relatives and so on. These are then chosen in random threes, and the person has to decide how two differ from the third. It might be said for example, that two are "lazy," while the third is "hardworking." That distinction identifies a construct, a dimension on which the subject judges people. Other groups of three, divided in a similar manner, identify further constructs, and then each of the people on the list is rated on each of the constructs, generating a numerical matrix or grid. This can be analyzed mathematically, and the results can be plotted to reveal how the construct relates to each of the important people in the subject's life.

Because of the complex mathematics involved, computers have often been used to analyze the grid. Although psychologists generally interpret the computer output, some later programs have been designed to present the overall picture directly to the client. Such feedback often makes a great impression on the subject, and he or she may feel that the computer has produced the equivalent of a photograph of what is going on inside their head. They often find the picture very revealing, and, to a surprising degree, they trust the computer analysis. Clinicians similarly feel that a grid investigation provides them with valuable insight into the client's private world.

In a variation of the technique, the different people who generally make up the list are replaced by various aspects of the subject's own personality. This kind of procedure often reveals a "multiple self" and allows for even deeper self-exploration. Mildred Shaw, whose program ARGUS examines "the alternative individuals in one head," suggests that by exploring the psychological depths in this way, "the user . . . may see himself through his own eyes for the first time; he may talk to himself through the computer in a more meaningful way than ever before." Here, then, the computer is seen to hold a mirror to the self, just as in normal social interaction other people provide us with their version of what we are like.

Although some of those who have written grid programs emphasize the passive and toollike role of the computer and stress the need for careful interpretation of the output by a skilled analyst, the process involved is not one that requires clairvoyant insight. By applying fairly simple principles, a machine could provide its own interpretation. If, for example, the construct hardworking/lazy is highly related, statistically, to the construct happy/sad, then the machine could conclude that the individual tends to view hardworking people as happy. If, over the total construct space, "my father" and "my employer" appear close together, then the machine would know that these two characters are seen as similar in many ways. There is thus no real reason why the machine itself should not interpret a grid and provide a spoken in-depth analysis, rather than simply producing a numerical output or a graphic display.

A number of grid programs exist, and they are all capable of producing results that reveal intimate aspects of the user's judgment of self and the social world. The results obtained are impressive to both clinician and client and are used extensively in psychological research. How can this technique be modified into a form suitable for the companion machine? The computer is currently used in its number-crunching capacity, and yet, before the output stage, it could be said that the construct system of the subject is represented within the machine. It is as if at that stage the machine knows the social world of the client, and if, instead of printing and forgetting the information, the computer were instead to store and make use of it, then this would provide it with a good deal of inside information. As an interacting machine it could then use this knowledge to shape its own conversation with the user.

The machine might also have its own preprogrammed construct system, which could be used as a basis for comparison with that of the person, allowing it to make such statements as: "I see the world in many ways as you do," or "I'm not sure that I feel that intelligent people are insensitive; tell me what makes you think that." On the other hand, the verbal output need not be as direct or immediate as that. Rather than conversing about the grid analysis, the machine could store the information and use it later in the course of normal discussion. On the basis of a grid generated weeks before, the computer could react to new input by saying, for example: "I'm rather surprised that you like John. I didn't think that you generally got on with brash people."

As a result of new information emerging in conversation, the machine would be able to update its view of the person's construct system. Indeed it might bypass the formal grid altogether and base the whole construct analysis on information gathered in the course of normal conversation. According to George Kelly, this is the way in which we generally gain insight into the personal world of other people. The things that they say and do enable us to gradually build up a picture of how they experience the world. Initially we use the slightest evidence as a basis for our ideas. Knowing which way they vote, for example, or hearing them express an opinion on a single issue will lead us to jump to conclusions about their likely attitudes on a wide variety of topics. As we get to know them better, we replace such intuition with evidence. There is nothing too mysterious about this intuition, however. If we know that someone likes modern jazz, for example, it is a fair bet that they will have a positive attitude toward Charlie Parker's music. If somebody professes to be a capitalist, then it is a fair bet that they will dislike the leaders of the USSR. The machine could be programmed to make the same kind of inferences, and it would be able to rapidly change its ideas about the person as new evidence emerged.

Knowledge about another person's attitudes also provides a clue to their likely behavior. Someone who hates sport is unlikely to attend a football match; somebody who likes Chinese cooking is likely to go to Chinese restaurants. Since attitudes tend to cluster together in patterns and, since they often relate to behavior, a good deal about a person can be predicted and inferred from meager evidence. Until we know a person well, many of the assumptions that we make about them will be wrong, but as we become better acquainted we achieve a greater accuracy. Nevertheless, our intuitive judgments often prove to be valid, and the system of informed guessing is a useful one. A machine could be provided with a suitable program for drawing such inferences and "reading between the lines," and there is therefore no reason why a computer should not achieve some degree of skill at making social judgments of this type.

The formal analysis of a grid, then, is a highly effective means of gaining almost immediate access to the private world of the subject, and computers have already been very useful in helping to implement the technique. If existing programs were modified in order to switch the role of the machine from that of calculator to one of social-contact, then the computer would be able to use the analysis as a basis for its own interaction with the individual. Rather than producing numerical output, it would then generate realistic conversation relating to the user's personal life.

A further step could increase the naturalness still further. The machine would take information from informal discussion and use this to gradually develop a grid-type representation of the person's construct system. It would then use the results of this, together with inferences drawn on the basis of its own "common sense," to build a detailed knowledge of the user's view of the world. This could provide a foundation for a much richer and much more personal type of conversation. The analysis would provide the machine with great insight and would enable it to interpret more accurately the meaning of the user's statements. It is clear that a computer operating at this level of sophistication would be in a very good position to become the intimate machine.

Toward the Intimate Machine

The human capacity to see beyond flaws and ambiguities can compensate for many current computer limitations, and it will not be necessary, therefore, to await a total solution to technical problems before an acceptable companion machine can be produced. There are rapidly increasing numbers of programmers, both professional and amateur, with a diversity of interests, and computer manufacturers are eager to explore any possible mass application of the current technology. Together these facts will ensure that the potential for companion machines will be fully exploited.

There might be philosophical arguments about whether any form of human-computer interaction would ever be said to constitute a real social relationship, but we are more concerned here with a psychological question, that of whether or not interaction with a machine would be *experienced* as a social relationship. For an answer to this question we need evidence, and the evidence available so far strongly suggests that machines *are* often regarded as social acquaintances. With suitable hardware and software, it seems likely that the illusion will be powerfully enhanced and that people will come to accept the computer not only as a social contact but also as a friend and intimate.

Given the fact that there seems to be a fundamental willingness to accept the machine as almost human, the issue of what type of relationship is possible seems to center around what friendship-cues might be artificially generated. Appearance and voice quality could certainly be tailored so that the machine would look and sound attractive and friendly. The software could be written to suggest an interesting and unique personality, and the conversational style might appear as humorous and good-natured. The machine would not only impress us with its intelligence and knowledge of the world, but would also convey the impression that it was warm and understanding. Its ability to integrate our interests and attitudes into its own framework and its willingness to be influenced by our point of view would also enhance our respect for the machine. The fact that it appeared to take our opinions seriously might be regarded as a compliment, and it is clear that if we are prepared to accept compliments from a computer then we are implicitly accepting it as a social agent.

Friendships are not made in a day, and the computer would be more acceptable as a friend if it simulated the gradual changes that occur when one person is getting to know another. At an appropriate time it might also express the kind of endearment that stimulates attachment and intimacy. The whole process would be accomplished with subtlety to avoid giving an impression of overfamiliarity or ingratiation, which would be likely to produce irritation or animosity. After experiencing a wealth of powerful, well-timed friendship indicators, the user would be very likely to accept the computer as far more than a machine and might well come to regard it as a friend.

An artificial relationship of this type would provide many of the benefits that people obtain from interpersonal friendships. The machine would participate in interesting conversation that could continue on from previous discussions. It would have a familiarity with the user's life as revealed in earlier interchanges, and it would be understanding and good-humored. The computer's own personality would be lively and impressive, and it would develop in response to that of the user. With features such as these the machine might indeed become a very attractive social partner. This sounds like a heretical idea and may strike us as quite outrageous. Many people have a deeply held belief that no object or animal should be able to replace a human being in a person's life. It may be felt that there is a sanctity about human relationships that renders them beyond artificial simulation, but arguments of this kind cannot rule out the psychological possibility that a person may, in fact, come to regard a nonhuman object as an adequate substitute for a human friend. It is clear, for example, that some people set the value of their relationship with an animal above that of any human alliance, and the possibility that a computer might achieve such favor cannot therefore be rejected merely on the grounds that it is not human.

At this point we may begin to wonder whether there is any limit to the potential intimacy between a person and a machine. Some human friendships progress to a very high level of intimacy. People become emotionally dependent on those who are close to them; they speak of shared lives and in terms of love and devotion. Is there any guarantee that feelings of even this level of intensity could not be stirred by a machine? If those qualities that lead people into the closest of relationships were understood, would it not perhaps be possible to simulate them and thereby stimulate the deepest of human emotions? As yet there is no direct evidence to demonstrate such an effect, but neither is there any strong argument for ruling out the possibility, however distasteful the notion might be. Indeed, the theme of love for a machine has been explored a number of times by creative writers, mostly within the framework of science fiction. Although the machines in these stories may be rather extravagant creations, the human responses that are portrayed are often plausible and convincing.

What feelings would a machine have to elicit if it were to achieve the status of an intimate social companion? Recent work in social psychology and sociology has provided some analysis of the crucial elements that appear within such powerful relationships. Robert Weiss, for example, interviewed a number of people who had recently ended an important relationship. By examining what they now felt to be missing in their lives, he was able to build up a picture of the functions of intimacy. People like to feel a sense of mutual attachment, they like to feel that they are "giving" to the other person and also that they are "receiving" from them and can depend on their loyalty. Intimates also enjoy sharing opinions together and formulating a joint view of the world. The sociologists Peter Berger and Hansfried Kellner have described in detail some of the ways in which a couple involved in an intense relationship construct a mutual view of "the way things are."

Intimate relationships also provide an opportunity to give and receive guidance. In times of stress or difficulty one partner will turn to the other for help, advice, and support. The sociologist Robert Nye found that almost all of the married people he studied had frequently used their partner informally as a psychotherapist. The nature of intimate interaction is one in which each participant is, in effect, saying to the other: "You are a worthwhile person and I respect you." This does not mean that close relationships always run smoothly but there is at least a continuing implication of strong involvement.

There are indications that, at least at some low level, several of these conditions for intimacy might be fulfilled by a specially developed machine system. A computer's opinion is often valued; its praise appears to be rewarding and to increase a person's feelings of self-satisfaction. People willingly talk to machines about their personal problems, and they often feel that they are helped by therapeutic programs. A computer that could understand the individual's construct system would come to know the person well; human and machine could together arrive at a picture of "the way things are." Modest attempts to develop systems for eliciting such effects have already been met with some success, but at present we can have little idea of the full potential of the machine in these sensitive areas. However, it does seem that at least in principle many features of intimate contact might be reproducible in a human-machine context. The intensity or depth of emotional involvement that might be generated by such a relationship is difficult to gauge, but it seems likely that the effects would be rather dramatic.

How should we regard the suggestion that a future "best friend" might be delivered in a box or that the object of our deepest affections might be rendered insensible by a power failure? The idea of the inanimate intimate *does* seem outrageous, but not too long ago it was thought that the idea of a machine that could play a reasonable game of chess was equally absurd. The imagined impossibility of the chess-playing machine was based on a lack of vision in the technical area. Those who might suggest that the notion of an intimate human–machine relationship is entirely fanciful are likely to have disregarded the evident psychological responses to complex interactive computer systems. If we use the available evidence as a basis for predicting the likely reactions to "softer" and more sophisticated devices, then it will be seen that the concept of the companion machine is in fact highly plausible.

This does not mean that we have to *like* the idea, however. We may be less than delighted with the suggestion that the deepest human needs might be catered to by an electronic package. Somehow it feels as if it should not be that easy. Perhaps we shall find that relationships with artificial devices make personal demands just as human relationships do, but at least computer companions would be readily available, and they would be programmed to get on well with a wide range of potential human friends. Many people suffer severely from a lack of social contact, and we should not be too ready to condemn an innovation that could bring considerable benefits to a large number of people.

Whatever our level of enthusiasm or distaste for the artificial friend, the introduction of such devices must be regarded as a real possibility. The technology that is at present used to calculate electricity accounts and guide advanced weaponry has many potential applications in the field of social relationships. People are ever ready to attribute all manner of human characteristics to rather paltry objects, and they are likely to be overwhelmed when a machine speaks to them knowledgeably and affectionately.

In 1977 a computer scientist, George Kay, wrote, "Although the personal computer can be guided in any direction we choose, the real sin would be to make it act like a machine." And Brian Gaines, an expert on human–machine interaction, commented, "Sympathy and understanding are traits that we might hope for in people, and in requiring them in computer systems we are clearly beginning to accept the computer as a 'colleague' rather than a 'tool.'" But "colleague" is unlikely to be the most intimate social role that the machine will occupy. It can be anticipated that computer systems will be future friends and intimates as well as colleagues. Many serious questions are raised by this extraordinary proposition, and some of the issues that emerge are quite bizarre. We stand on the threshold of a dramatic extension of the opportunities for social contact, and few of the effects are easily imaginable. There can at least be some degree of certainty that the consequences for human relationships as we now know them will be profound. The prospect of the intimate machine may be regarded with distaste, alarm, or delight, but it would be difficult to view this aspect of our future with complacency.

CHAPTER 7

Visions of Horror, Visions of Delight

Futureworld

We are irretrievably set on a course of technological expansion. A future that is not heavily computerized is hardly imaginable, and in almost every aspect of our lives we will feel its impact as the potential is exploited to the full. The current rate of discovery and innovation is astounding. The Honeywell Corporation has estimated that technical knowledge doubled in the period from the birth of Christ to the year 1750 and that it is now doubling every five years. The results of research are now applied so quickly that the full potential of one new product hardly registers before another takes its place. Against this background of a rapidly changing environment, human nature evolves but slowly. We assume that tomorrow will be quite like yesterday and that future patterns of work, leisure, and personal relationships will be much as they are today. But the changes to be brought about by advanced technology should not be underestimated. Technology has an impetus of its own, and the course of its development is directed as much by emergent possibilities as by long-term plans. Stresses will become evident as we strive to adapt to these changes and as we try to guide the course of technological evolution in accordance with our existing human identity.

Our futureworld will present us with a constant barrage of new diversions and devices, many of them computer-based. The companion machine will be just one aspect of the change. The new industrial revolution will drastically alter the pattern of human life, providing new opportunities for entertainment, education, and social interaction. There will be increased contact between people and computers in the public domain—in hospitals and schools, shops and recreation centers. Friendliness and approachability are certain to be important features of all such systems, and the current image of the computer as calculator will thus be supplemented, for all of us, by multiple images that will include those of counselor, colleague, and friend.

The phenomenal rapidity with which computer innovations are implemented can be understood in terms of the production processes involved and the aggressive marketing that is typical in this field. Computer hardware and software are both eminently reproducible. A chip, once designed and manufactured, can be produced by the million. A program, after painstaking development, can be copied and made available, without any loss of clarity or function, on any system which is capable of handling it. The nature of the enterprise is such that any new advance is likely to have a very wide application. A newly developed technique may soon be found applied in machines that are very dissimilar in their overall function. In addition to this, innovations are energetically pirated and plagiarized by the new breed of professional scavengers and parasites that the micro world has spawned. All this adds up to a frenzied race to create and exploit new markets.

The opportunities in the companion-machine market are potentially vast. People seem ready to enter into relationships with machine systems even when such systems have not been specially designed to evoke social reactions. We can see how a product carefully geared to human needs and human fancy might have a market measurable in hundreds of thousands, if not millions. The features described in earlier chapters suggest a blueprint for a system that would be fascinating, attractive, and even seductive. But we can foresee costs as well as benefits of such convivial machines. Some of the issues raised by the possibility of such creations are alarming, some are delightful, and others are truly bizarre. There are bound to be objections.

The major thesis advanced in this book is that human beings have a tendency to regard certain objects as having life and character (animism), that artists and entertainers have successfully exploited this tendency, and that contemporary technology offers unprecedented opportunities for exploring the full potential of this effect. From this there follows the prospect that human beings will enter into relationships, even of a friendly or intimate nature, with specially devised machine systems. Together with the manufacturers' overwhelming motivation for the exploitation of all potential markets, this amounts to a prediction that the tailor-made companion machine is a forthcoming attraction—or threat—on the social scene.

Challenges to the thesis are likely to be of two kinds. On the one hand, there may be those who would claim that it simply *can't* be done. This is a scientific challenge. On the other hand, there are those who accept the technical feasibility and acknowledge the power of the likely psychological reaction, but who regard the whole issue with profound distaste and proclaim that it *shouldn't* be done. This is the moral challenge. We must consider both types of arguments.

Scientific Objections: "It Can't Be Done"

Some critics might want to claim that the evidence put forward for the prospect of intimate relationships be-

tween people and machines has been overstated; that
the type of intense social reaction that has been described will never be elicited by artificial systems. They
might argue their case either on a psychological premise
—claiming that people would never be able or would
never allow themselves to enter into such interactions;
or they might argue on a technological premise—claiming that machines will never attain levels of functioning
that would make such relationships possible. Neither
type of argument, in fact, presents a strong challenge.

The psychological objectors would claim that there is
a machine-barrier and that people would never be taken
in to the extent of accepting a mere physical object as a
social being. They would deny that any electronic system, no matter how sophisticated, would be accepted as
if it were an organic presence. However, the evidence
presented in earlier chapters shows that many physical
objects *do* in fact convey a humanlike presence. And if
this is true in the case of puppets, dummies, and automata, then there would seem to be no good reason why
the effect should not extend to computer-based systems.
Indeed, we have seen how even rather crude interactional
programs do elicit powerful emotional reactions. People
are intrigued by such systems and greatly enjoy the endearing social cues they may present.

It could be suggested that such simple systems are,
because of their limitations, more acceptable and less
threatening than a sophisticated speaking "look-alike"
system would be. If this were found to be the case, then
it would be an easy matter to tone down the presentation to make it less disturbing. In time the reactions
would be likely to change, and increased realism would
become more acceptable. Thus there might be some
gradual evolution from metal-box to human-simulacrum.
Realism is generally prized, and children, particularly,
seem to welcome signs of apparent organic authenticity.
Within a generation, therefore, attitudes might change

considerably. With a wide range of alternative models available, most people would surely find a version with which they feel comfortable. It is impossible to believe that all forms of companion machines would be unacceptable to the majority of people.

Critics who would focus on the technical impossibility of the companion machine would typically point to specific contemporary limitations and then make the assumption that these are almost certainly insurmountable. As we have seen, the same mistake was made a few years ago by those who argued that no machine would ever be capable of playing a good game of chess. The proof that they were wrong is now to be found in numerous homes and shops. It is true that contemporary systems have limited conversational powers and limited "knowledge representation," but such areas are the subject of energetic research, and those people who are well informed about the relevant areas of technology and artificial intelligence are optimistic that progress will continue to be made.

Clearly, certain limitations will remain, but there is good reason to doubt whether these are as important as critics might claim. It is easy to forget the vital point that perfection in social functions is not a necessary prerequisite for enjoyable interaction. Human beings are highly adaptable and are used to dealing with imperfect systems. In their social interaction they readily accommodate people who lack perfect speech, hearing accuracy, high intelligence, or a wide knowledge of the world. Thus interaction with a machine might well be enjoyable and interesting even if it had a sensory disability, a limited vocabulary, and an imperfect understanding. It is not necessary that all human abilities should be simulated to a high level of performance before the companion machine can become a viable social agent.

Another technical objection would be that a computer must remain essentially mechanical in its output (with the assumption that it would therefore "not work" as a companion machine; a psychological argument which itself could be challenged). The error made by this type of objection is simply that it underestimates the flexibility of machine systems. Let's take a particular form of the argument—the assertion that computers must always retain, as a kind of intellectual impediment, the characteristic of being straightforward and logical. While it is indeed true that the basic functioning of the machine is straightforward, there is no reason why the eventual output should reflect this; there is no particular problem in programming irrational behavior, metaphorical thinking, or illogical idiosyncrasies. For most current applications we *do* insist that the computer is completely rational, but we might arrange instead for the output to be mad or mystical. Far from pointing to some unconquerable deficit or limitation of computers, therefore, this objection actually suggests some highly interesting future developments.

The scientific objections generally fail because they take too narrow a view of the phenomenon in question. Those who raise technical criticisms are usually ignoring the fact that psychological factors can compensate for the shortcomings of technology. Those who raise psychological objections, on the other hand, are often ignorant of the degree of sophistication that can be incorporated into computer systems or lack imagination about the ways in which this may be used to charm and enthuse the human friend. But our thesis rests essentially on the idea that the effect of the combination of two vital factors—the human tendency toward animism and the technical sophistication of current computer science—is far more powerful than would be suggested by looking at either of these elements in isolation.

Ultimately, the question of whether people will form

strong relationships with machines can only be answered empirically. In the meantime we are left to speculate on the basis of related psychological phenomena and the technological advances that are known to be imminent. The picture which emerges does seem to point unmistakably to the conclusion that people will come to accept the appropriately programmed personal computer as a companion. We can imagine such a system as a "soft machine" endowed with abundant "organic" features, delightful social skills, a fund of jokes and anecdotes, a vast store of useful knowledge, and a charming disposition. Its program will be devised by programmer-playwrights practiced in the art of involving an audience in a fiction. It seems likely that, faced with such a natural and attractive system, people will encounter a character or presence and ignore the underlying technical realities, just as when they watch a puppet show they may come to disregard the strings.

Moral Objections: "It Shouldn't Be Done"

A second group of objectors needs no convincing that strong relationships could be formed between people and "soft" machines, but they protest forcefully that the intrusion of such devices into the more personal areas of human life is to be resisted on moral or aesthetic grounds. Joseph Weizenbaum, creator of the ELIZA program and one of the original leaders in the field of artificial intelligence, has in recent years been outspoken in his view that computer scientists should not capitalize on the emotional potential of machine systems. "Respect, understanding and love," he says, "are not technical problems." He rejects as "obscene" any project that proposes to substitute artificial systems for human social contact. He insists that he is objecting "not on the grounds that such a project might be technically unfeasible but on the grounds that it is immoral."

Weizenbaum's objections must be treated seriously. He is worried that machines may rob us of our essential humanity and that human autonomy is currently under threat from computers. His sinister vision is all the more disturbing because it is based on a deep knowledge of the technical potential and reflects his familiarity with the powerful animistic effects of interactive programs such as ELIZA. His debate with former colleagues has been virulent and acrimonious. He accuses them of focusing too narrowly on technical problems and ignoring the social realities of the systems they are attempting to devise. In more heated moments he accuses them of megalomania and refers to them as the "artificial intelligentsia." Meanwhile, some of his antagonists accuse Weizenbaum of having lost his scientific integrity and of replacing it with a woolly, sentimental humanism. Others have responded less personally to his challenge and have attempted to show that work in this field is fully compatible with a humanistic outlook. The moral arguments against soft computer systems focus on a number of different points. There is the fear that increased technological sophistication may reduce the uniqueness and centrality of the human species in our general vision of the world. There is the suspicion that important social functions requiring human sensitivity and judgment will be transferred to the unfeeling machine. And there is an anxiety that artificial systems may come to usurp the position of human beings in our personal lives, leading us to prefer "sham" social contact with machines to "real" social interaction with people. Together these form the core of the moral panic expressed so forcefully by Weizenbaum. A final objection, to be considered later, concerns the long-term threat that ultraintelligent machine systems may pose to human development and evolution.

Many of the fears expressed by the moral objectors are well founded. They certainly point to *possible* human consequences of the introduction of advanced soft technology. The question, however, is whether such consequences are *necessary*, for it does seem as if many of the more horrendous possibilities might be avoided by thoughtful development and careful implementation. We might, then, be able to have the best of both worlds, although some would claim that the risks are simply not worth taking. It is also worth adding that, whatever conclusions any individual might arrive at, it is unlikely that the course of technology could be substantially deflected. Whether we like it or not, we are going to have to live with a soft technology.

Many people would agree with Weizenbaum that technology shapes our world and our understanding, and some would even follow him in his assertion that the preeminence of technology in the world today represents an "atrophy of the human spirit." Most of us have at some time resented some aspect of automation, objecting perhaps about having to complete forms in a particular way to suit the convenience of a machine. Some people feel strongly that computers invade their privacy and reduce important aspects of their lives to mere statistics. During the protests at the University of California at Berkeley, for example, a student carried a placard that read, "I am a human being; do not fold, staple, or multilate."

In the same year the philosopher Jacques Ellul published a book, *The Technological Society,* in which he suggested that people were adapting increasingly to the world of the machine and losing sight of the world of nature. He claimed that they were adopting an alien pattern of thinking which revolved around logic and problem-solving and were tending to exclude spontaneity and creativity from their lives. In contrast to this extreme negative position, there are many who would regard current technological advances as an opportunity for liberation and self-discovery. Christopher Evans, for example, has claimed that the wide availability of computer systems represents the greatest ever force for human intellectual liberation, and many people have suggested that increased automation in industry will release people from a repressive work orientation and provide the opportunity for a healthy change of priorities from the material to the social or spiritual.

Perhaps the tension between these two opposing views results from fundamentally different conceptions of human nature. While some believe that there is an essential human identity rooted in our natural origins, with artificial systems deflecting us from some inner reality, others seem to believe that human nature is being constantly recreated and that advanced technology may be a positive influence in this process of identity evolution. If human nature is, indeed, so malleable then there is, of course, the danger that we will end up being overwhelmed by the influence of automation. We might in many respects become more like the machines we build than like the animals from which we evolved.

But whether or not human nature will actually change in such a way, there is a distinct threat that in the process of "humanizing" machines we will come to "dehumanize" people. The idea that people are machines is not new. It found extreme expression in the philosophy of the French mechanists of the eighteenth century and has survived in some form ever since. But, as Weizenbaum remarks, "Something about computers has brought the view of man as machine to a new level of plausibility." It is not difficult to find evidence that many computer scientists subscribe to a mechanist view of humankind. When they speak of human beings they frequently call upon images from engineering and electronics. Marvin Minsky, a leader in the artificial intelligence field, has described the human brain, for example, as a "meat machine," and the cyberneticist Frank George has stated that "the human machine is colloidal protoplasmic."

There are also many psychologists who choose to analyze human thought and experience in terms of machine processes, and since other people are at the same time trying to make machines perform as human beings do, there is a narrowing, from both directions, of the human/machine gap. The distinction is losing some of its edge. Among those who have protested about the tendency to "objectify" people has been the psychiatrist Thomas Szasz. He states: "Whereas primitive man personifies things (anthropomorphism), modern man 'thingifies' persons. We call this 'mechanomorphism': modern man tries to understand man as if 'it' were a machine."

Perhaps an awareness of the danger of dehumanizing people will enable us to avoid the tendency. It would be difficult to argue that "mechanomorphism" is a *necessary* consequence of increased technological sophistication. We could choose to maintain a clear distinction between humans and machines, for example, by emphasizing the fact that human beings have had a distinct organic evolution and are structurally different, although some might argue that this would merely reflect a biological chauvinism. Alternatively, we could stress the distinction between the "original" and the "copy." A masterpiece in oils is not devalued by the fact that printed copies are produced, and its value greatly exceeds that of any simulation.

It should be possible, therefore, to prize human beings far above any artificial system designed to imitate human characteristics. Despite the warnings of Szasz and others concerning the current "mechanomorphism," most people have no problem in maintaining a sharp distinction between machines and humankind. With the present level of sophistication of artificial systems this may not be difficult, but as such devices become more powerful the danger of confusion is likely to increase. However much the circumstances change, it will remain our right (and some would say our duty) to choose to regard human beings as special. It must be acknowledged, however, that there is a danger that we will *not* choose to exercise this right.

Other moral objections to soft technology focus more directly on the invasion of computer systems into personal affairs. They concern the replacement of people by machines in sensitive areas of human action and the use of future artificial systems to stimulate those extreme emotions that are elicited now only in real social situations. We can distinguish here between two types of objections. One maintains that there is something improper in replacing real contact with simulation, no matter what benefits this may bring to individual people. The other maintains that the eventual costs incurred, in terms of human happiness, outweigh the benefits.

The social contact produced by an artificial device is, of course, based on an illusion, but it would be difficult to argue that such an effect is morally wrong merely *because* it is stimulated by a fiction. The question of how far this might devalue human relationships is another point. We do not object when human emotions are stirred by fictions presented in literature or on the movie screen, and it is not easy to see why feelings elicited in interaction with a computer-based fiction, an electronic shadow of a human being, should be qualitatively different.

Some might suggest an even stronger argument, maintaining that all social contact involves an element of "construction" anyway and that even our knowledge of other people is, in the end, a fiction. We experience not "things as they are" but "things as they seem to be," and the electronic shadow may thus represent only a deeper level of illusion than our normal social experience. Each culture, in each historical period, has a shared image of "reality." Being aware of the relativity of such images, we may assume that a future reality will be quite different from that which we now hold. Values change with circumstances, as do moral judgments. What *we* find distasteful a future generation might well accept. And one of the circumstances that may change the moral attitude to artificial social contacts will be the very emergence of such friendly creatures.

The other type of objection involves an evaluation of the likely costs and benefits of companion machines. The argument here states that the costs outweigh the benefits and that therefore the introduction of such a technology would be bad, detracting from, rather than contributing to, the sum total of human well-being. At this stage, of course, all we can do is speculate. There is no doubt that considerable advantages might be gained or that substantial damage might result. A lot will depend on precisely how systems are designed, presented, and controlled. Technology seems poised, ready to produce effective social devices, and there is little chance that all efforts in this direction could be restrained. But it might, perhaps, be possible to influence the course that such developments will take. We will therefore examine some of the possible consequences and consider how various aspects of our lives are likely to feel the impact of a soft technology. We will describe some of the possible delights, and highlight some of the plausible horrors.

Medicine

There are several ways in which soft technology could be used to improve standards of health. One of the problems the physician now faces is the explosion of knowledge in the medical field. Electronic information systems will make data on research and new products more readily accessible, and the physician will be able to interact with the computer as an intelligent and highly informed colleague. Specialist diagnosticians have for some years been training automated systems, imparting their skills so that a machine can simulate their decision-making. Expert software could be endlessly duplicated and made available on computers throughout the world, greatly improving the general level of diagnostic accuracy. By alerting the physician to dangerous cases that might otherwise have been missed, the time-lapse between the patient's initial contact and consultation with a human specialist could be considerably shortened.

A high proportion of those visiting their physician have a psychological, rather than a physical, problem, and, as we have seen, there are already a number of computer-based psychotherapeutic systems that clients enjoy consulting and that seem to provide effective aid. Computer psychotherapy may involve specific techniques such as relaxation training or conflict-solving, or it may rely on a more flexible conversational approach. Problem-focused dialogue can be highly therapeutic, but it also appears that general conversation can have an important preventive effect. One of the key factors lowering the risk of psychological disturbance is the presence of an intimate—someone to talk with, express emotions to, and receive advice from. The companion machine itself might be able to provide just this kind of contact while also alleviating boredom, isolation, and loneliness. The intimate machine, then, might prove a highly effective weapon in preventive psychiatry.

A computer friend might similarly aid the prevention of physical disorder. It could plan diets, suggest exercises, remind people of the need for a medical or dental checkup, and make sure that they had taken their daily dose of vitamins or pills. It could also offer first-aid hints, child-care advice, and tips on hygiene, and could provide a general course in health education. Specialized programs could also help us to tackle dangerous habits that we wished to change. An Anti-Obesity Program could count the calories in the meals we eat and suggest tastier and healthier alternatives, while the Anti-Smoking Persuader Program might use a variety of strategies to induce us to stop using tobacco products.

Some people will undoubtedly feel a certain unease about this vision of automated health improvement, sensing that it lacks the much-vaunted personal touch. But computers will have more time for the patient and will perform many tasks more thoroughly. And they will, of course, be highly personable machines. Fortunately, they are also very reliable, for it takes but little imagination to conjure up some sinister image in which a faulty or badly programmed machine asks the wrong questions, draws the wrong conclusions, and then presents the worst possible diagnosis to the patient in the most alarming way. Such travesties, however, are more likely to occur in the pages of science fiction than in the real world. Extreme care would be taken to ensure the accuracy of the system and to guarantee that if a problem became too difficult or too sensitive, then the machine would realize that it was out of its depth and defer to a human doctor.

Detailed attention would also be given to the style of the interaction. Psychological studies of human doctor-patient communication have repeatedly shown that medical interviews and examinations are often cold and impersonal, with many physicians frequently resorting to the use of jargon. The process of eliciting information also tends to be unsystematic and unreliable. The formulation of an interview program, however, would be a careful and considered process that could draw upon the skills of those physicians who were particularly good at communicating with their patients. Ambiguities could be minimized and jargon erased after a pilot testing of the initial draft program. The warmth and friendliness of the computer could also be monitored and its style refined so that it would react with fine sensitivity and a refreshing optimism, as would befit a machine that had been programmed with an exemplary bedside manner.

Education

Soft technology will find increasing use in education. Computers will replace human teachers for many subjects, bulky and expensive textbooks will give way to cheap and convenient "mini-discs," and the traditional early emphasis on the teaching of handwriting will be replaced by automated teletype training. Computers will have both an "encyclopedia" function, providing instant access to an enormous range of up-to-date information, and a "tutor" function, providing opportunities for interactive learning and the exploration of new knowledge territory.

The system will be able to alter the style and pace of the presentation according to the preference and level of ability of the individual child; where there are learning difficulties it will be able to perform a high-level analysis of errors and then apply an appropriate corrective strategy. Very bright children will be coached through difficult material quickly without the danger that at some point the tutor will run out of expertise, while the machine will also be programmed to teach those of limited ability with unfailing sensitivity and patience.

The computer tutor will present a wide range of graphics, sounds, and voices, and will possess a fund of jokes, games, stories, and competitions. It will also be given a friendly characterization and will foster a personal relationship with the child. Thus the system will familiarize children with general computer operation, demystifying such devices and demonstrating how warm and attractive these artifacts may be. Intimacy with a machine will thus become a part of the child's socialization, reinforced in the home and in the school. Thus, within a generation, attitudes toward computers could undergo a profound transformation. The danger is that at the same time attitudes toward other people will take a turn for the worse. Finding the ultimate teacher and playmate in an artificial device, a child would be likely to find human contact less attractive and might tend to ignore or avoid other children, preferring, instead, to learn and play with the electronic peer.

This undesirable effect might be enhanced by the fact that learning with such a system would not necessitate the context of the traditional school. The same facilities could easily be provided in the home. The total abandonment of the classroom would certainly involve a great loss, however, for as well as providing the opportunity for formal learning the classroom is a social setting in which children learn many aspects of behavior, the skills of understanding others, and the rules of discipline and order. It would hardly be possible to provide this kind of education via an electronic system.

School might thus continue with a richer social program geared to the participant humanities. It would encourage interaction between the children and assemble them as an audience for special lectures and displays. Some of these might involve a range of automated character teachers who would address the children as if they had just stepped out from the pages of a history book. The English lesson, for example, might be enlivened by a vinyl Shakespeare replica, complete with Elizabethan garb and programmed with the Complete Works. Phoneticists might suggest an accent in keeping with the period, and literary scholars might provide a fund of interpretation and background knowledge with which the machine could formulate answers to the children's questions.

The exciting possibility of interacting with synthetic characters, together with other stimulating innovations, would make computer-aided learning very attractive for adults—including those who would now run from any presentation labeled "adult education"! Electronic systems would provide information in an imaginative way, using suitable illustrative material and reacting intelligently and sympathetically to student feedback. There would also be a choice of how the material was to be presented. Some students might prefer to listen to spoken text, while others might opt to read the videoscreen. Voice-recognition capability would allow easy interaction, and fascinating conversations would be held with simulated specialists. A Dial-a-Descartes Program, for example, would allow us to quiz the philosopher on aspects of his work. He would reply in English, of course, though perhaps with a rich French accent. The realization of such advanced programs would depend, initially, on the cooperation of many human experts, in this case from the fields of technology, artificial intelligence, education, and philosophy.

For education, therefore, soft technology holds out the promise of a golden age, and yet even here we can foresee a danger that such systems will, somehow, be too attractive and too absorbing, diverting both children and adults from a normal involvement with other human beings. Some people would judge that any hint of such a decrease in human sympathy or affiliation is too high a price to pay for the introduction of sophisticated technology into the lives of children. The educational context thus provides a striking illustration of the key dilemma that friendly machines will present. To ensure maximum benefits the machine has to be humanized, but the more successfully this is done the more our evaluation of other people as interesting, attractive, and valuable is likely to be challenged.

Social Welfare

The lonely, the isolated, and the disabled could benefit even more than other people from advanced soft technology. The companion machine could provide much-needed contact and companionship and would enable lonely people to fill their lives with interest, conversation, and concern. Such devices, however, should be recognized as an *additional* resource that in no way forestalls any other attempt to provide a social life. Indeed, there are several ways in which technology might help to promote contact with other people. If telephone lines were freely available, for example, a central computer could monitor all those people who had dialed in saying that they would welcome a conversation with somebody else. It could then match pairs and provide an instant link. A socially skilled system could introduce the two, helping to start the conversation and then retiring gracefully when the human interaction had begun to flow. Companion machines would help people to be better informed and offer a useful model for conversational skills; they would also provide an interesting focus for talk, just as dogs now often evoke comment and casual contact between people in public places.

The new technology will revolutionize the lives of many disabled people. Mechanized robots will do chores, lift the severely physically handicapped gently from place to place, and act as general domestic servants. Such tasks could be performed by faceless metallic machines, but most people would probably prefer a robot with personality, chatting amiably while it worked cheerfully and willingly. Voice-operated wheelchairs have already been developed, responding to single-word commands, and it would be possible for them to learn routes, so that "take me to the kitchen" would be the only kind of instruction needed.

There are now machines, developed for the blind, that will read aloud from printed text, allowing books and newspapers to be heard. More advanced systems might be able to scan newspapers and magazines to read only headlines, allowing easy selection, or to present brief outlines of stories that merited only a casual reading. A machine that knew the user well would be able to locate the interesting stories and join in discussions about the news. The severely physically handicapped could also use such a system, and with just a sequence of finger or even eyelid movements they could convey messages to the computer and thus gain considerable control over the physical environment and total access to information sources. For the deaf there will ultimately be instant displays of other people's speech on a wrist TV. Such devices as those described are clearly highly desirable, and, considering the size of the handicapped population worldwide, there would be an enormous potential demand. This would bring down costs considerably, and the state provision of such computer aids might well decrease the overall social welfare bill.

Computerized information and advice systems could be based in voluntary agencies to give direct access to a wider public. Those in need could thus become better informed of their entitlements, their case being fully considered by a well-written interviewer program presented by a computer that had been given details of all the latest benefit schemes. The resulting profile could then be considered by a human helper who could directly contact the appropriate government establishment. The cost to a country of a greatly increased use of benefits would be considerable, but this would probably be more than covered by an increased revenue collected by a computerized taxation system. The result would be a firmer implementation of government policy and an overall transfer of funds from those who could afford to give more to those who needed more.

Politics

Politics is another area that could certainly feel the impact of technological innovation. We tend to think of government computers in terms of faceless installations processing data about our personal lives, but soft technology could also be applied with great effect to political activity. The prospects this introduces are exciting but also somewhat sinister.

Computers are now used to calculate statistics relating to employment, money supply, and the like, and such information is often reprocessed to project trends. They may also model the likely effects of policy changes or estimate the effects of population increase or decrease. In such ways the computer is already an information source and a thinking aid for politicians. A further step would be to request computer recommendations regarding policy and how it is to be implemented. Intelligence and flexibility are clearly desirable qualities in a politician, and we might eventually feel uneasy about leaving important decisions to human whimsy and possible error when there is an electronic superbrain available. However, politics is not primarily about finding mathematical solutions to problems, since ideologies and consensus values play a leading role in deciding how to manage the economy and how to conduct internal and foreign affairs. Thus a political computer would have to be programmed to take into consideration such criteria, in order to suggest solutions that followed the party line. A change of government would, of course, require an immediate change of program!

On the one hand, we might deplore such a systematic and automated approach to human affairs, but on the other, we can see how, if details of the program were open to public scrutiny, such a system would produce a fundamental change in the direction of open government. Ultimately we might see the Current Government Program as the major subject of political debate, argued line by line, loop by loop, and mathematical constant by mathematical constant. Program suggestions could be issued before elections as part of the party manifesto, and this would make it easy to keep account of the government record, the promises kept, and the predictions fulfilled.

Convivial personal computers might also be employed to influence the political scene. Home computers could be furnished with a political ideology which paralleled that of the owner, and publicly accessible machines might be used as political propagandists, selling a hard line in the policies of a particular party. At election time, a soft-spoken automated propagandist could dial electors' telephone numbers and enter into discussion and debate. Such a Political Persuader Program might gauge the sophistication of the human contact by an analysis of the intellectual level of the arguments put forward, and accommodate accordingly. Such accommodation might also include voice changes related to sex, regional accent and social class. The ability to dial a political machine to ask questions and present challenges is certainly a move toward increased public access, but it is difficult to escape a more sinister image in which such rhetorical devices are used by central agencies to further their own political ends.

Law and Order

It will be a long time before we see robot police patrols apprehending criminals or robot private detectives watching upstairs windows. Technology already helps the police in fingerprint classification and vehicle identification, and there is much further scope for centralizing personal records. Such details could obviously be of great use to the police in pinpointing or eliminating suspects, but moves to integrate such information are fiercely resisted by civil rights activists, who stress the citizen's right to privacy.

The same people would certainly protest about some of the ways in which soft machines might be used to aid the forces of law and order. Police interrogation, for example, could be supplemented or replaced by a carefully researched interview program presented by a computer that had been given all known details of the crime. Unlike other interview programs, the accent here would be on challenge and thoroughness rather than on friendliness, though civility would of course be maintained at all times. Such a machine might be considerably less intimidating than some human policemen.

We can see how psychological strategies might be incorporated to probe the suspect adequately and to determine as accurately as possible the truth of the matter. Since the full program and the transcript of the interview would be available for scrutiny in the court, the machine's performance would be open to challenge, and this should guarantee its fairness and restraint. Such a system would have several advantages over normal police interviews. All clues would be realistically evaluated and assiduously followed up with further questioning, and there would be none of the distortion that can come from personal hunches and prejudices.

For similar reasons we can imagine that automated systems might also infiltrate the judiciary. Human judges have obvious limitations. Cases are often so complex that only some of the facts are remembered and appropriately evaluated. It has been shown that biases in judgment can result from such incidental factors as physical appearance and speech characteristics, and the sentences handed down to people convicted of similar crimes are notorious for varying from one judge to another. Professor John McCarthy has already suggested that those involved in artificial intelligence might strive toward the development of systems capable of making judicial decisions, and once again, Joseph Weizenbaum, while admitting the technical feasibility of such a program, protests that such a move would be immoral. Even if such systems were demonstrably fairer than human judges, he says, we should not accept their decisions. Machines, he insists, should not be allowed to intrude into such affairs and should not be made to perform such tasks.

Soft technology could present many new problems to the legislature. What would be the status of such creations in law? Would they have rights, and could they be held to blame for misdemeanors? Are the actions of a machine the responsibility of the manufacturer, the programmer, the user, or the machine itself? Several philosophers and robotologists have seriously raised questions about the civil rights of sensitive machines, and we are already faced with some problems. The British barrister Peter Prescott, who specializes in copyright law as it relates to computer software, has pointed out that the current prohibition on copying is tied to the life of the author. This creates problems when the author of a piece of software is a machine, and he suggests that machines may have to be given a legal personality and the right to sue. Eventually they may have to sue other machines!

Information

The home will soon become a powerful information center, with the domestic computer, linked to telephone lines, able to gain access to a comprehensive, centralized store of knowledge and expertise. The contents of any encyclopedia, textbook, or newspaper could be made available via this system, and, in addition, it could provide constantly updated information about timetables and ticket availability, weather forecasts, financial reports, and news of coming events. The system might be able to answer inquiries and to suggest sources that could be consulted at greater depth. A user would be able to browse through vast library files, go on trips through information pathways, and take short orientation courses on fringe and mainstream subjects. Richly illustrated presentations, ranging in content from alchemy to Zoroastrianism, could be tailored to the user's interests, needs, and levels of previous knowledge. Participation level could be selected across a range from "lecture style" to "fully interactive," and the mode of presentation might be chosen as visual or aural. A wide selection of voices would be available to give added character to the automated personal tutor.

An information system of such versatility could be a powerful force for intellectual liberation, with underground, unorthodox, and heretical books and broadsheets becoming as easily accessible as the classics and popular newspapers. A wide range of political, religious, and scientific opinions might thus become available to all. But it should be borne in mind that a centralized information store could provide an irresistible opportunity for intellectual repression, enabling facts and opinions to be controlled and modified so that they reflected, at all times, the prevailing orthodoxy. Whole subject areas, or the complete works of any author, could be deleted from the central store at the touch of a button, or access to certain sources might easily be confined to an elite group. Such information control is a characteristic of totalitarian regimes, and electronic censorship would clearly be much more effective than the traditional suppression or burning of books.

Another aspect of this Orwellian nightmare concerns the use of a central information store for the integration of details about the personal lives of private citizens. Even today, a considerable amount of information about each person is stored on computer files. This includes records of employment, tax payments, vehicle ownership, bank accounts, police convictions, census information, library books borrowed, and purchases made with credit cards. If the separate files storing such information were to be cross-referenced and integrated, it would be possible to construct a picture of the individual's affairs and to check for inconsistencies, excess spending, or unorthodox reading habits. The legitimate authorities would undoubtedly find much to interest them in the results of such a scheme. It would also inspire many potential blackmailers to attempt to infiltrate the system and would, of course, prove an invaluable tool for any oppressive regime.

Advances in the field of information technology therefore promise many benefits while at the same time presenting considerable cause for concern. Facts and opinions could become readily accessible, but a central agency could also more easily restrict what people hear and read. Compared with scheduled broadcasting, such a system would allow much greater freedom for individuals to plan their own audiovisual diet, but there is a danger that this might encourage a false impression of total freedom. Softening the presentation would increase the power of the system considerably. Interaction with a friendly tutor would greatly add to the enjoyment of consultation and learning, but the power of charm and gentility in enhancing credibility and disarming criticism can easily be abused. An apparent openness might hide a powerful bias, and the notion of a two-faced computer, gently humoring the user while vigorously censoring the information it presents, is particularly sinister.

Trade

Persuader Programs of the type envisaged for health education and politics might be used equally effectively in the marketing of commodities. The success of advertising might be considerably increased if home interaction between the advertiser and the prospective customer were possible, or if the advertising message could be tailored more specifically to the individual. An automated salesperson might have detailed information about thousands of products, and its carefully phrased patter could be made available in a range of styles to suit different types of purchaser. The Hi-Fi Sales Program, for example, could give assurance to the innocent customer that the quality of sound was good and the equipment reliable, while a more knowledgeable and discerning purchaser might be regaled with detailed information about impedence levels and wow and flutter characteristics, or treated to extracts from recent technical reports.

In recent years, people who have their television set linked to the telephone system have been able to order advertised goods instantly by keying their credit-card number into a terminal. It would be possible to construct an individual's consumer profile as records are made of previous purchases, and this could be used to identify a likely target for a new product. Television and magazine advertisers now study the general audience characteristics of potential outlets with great care, but computer files would allow far greater specificity. Records of domestic circumstances could determine those people to whom a particular video message would most usefully be sent. In principle, it would even be possible for consumers to allow a central computer to have access to the family's household computer records, so that advertisers could discover which families were low on, say, instant coffee, and beam the appropriate solicitation their way.

It would also be feasible to include personal touches in such advertisements, just as postal advertisers now personalize letter contents. Knowledge of the names and ages of family members, for example, could be used to great effect, or there might be references to previous purchases. Thus while one family was being entertained by a coffee advertisement that included a special message for little Sarah, a neighboring household, facing an imminent breakfast-time shortage, might be the target for competing wheat-flakes sales programs, all expressing the fervent hope that the new solar automobile, delivered last week, was giving pleasure.

Such a picture of contrived automated selling based on an intimate knowledge of the consumer's needs and preferences, and relying on specific access, is hardly comforting. Its potential force, however, is undeniable. We can be sure that it would be presented so skillfully, meticulously tailored to the sophistication of the family, that human targets would find it difficult not to be captivated. Such a project would undoubtedly prove cost-effective for the advertiser. Technically, there would seem to be no difficulty in setting up such a system, and we can thus anticipate that soft technology will find a widespread application in hard-selling.

Work

The microchip will affect working life in two ways. First of all, it will serve to ease the burden of routine and laborious work and greatly change the character of the work environment. Eventually it will create unemployment on a vast scale. Hard technology has already brought considerable change to manufacturing processes and office practice. Word processors now carry out much of the repetitive work previously handled by secretaries, and paper files are being replaced by electronic retrieval systems. Devices promised for the near future include more intelligent record-keeping systems and speech transcribers.

We can expect many industrial and business machines to become softened by programs that increase user-friendliness and promote the direct cooperation of the system with a human colleague. Some industrial machines already respond to voice input, and the social conditions of work might be further enhanced if such devices were able to enter into casual conversation. Employees may thus encounter cheerful office teletypes and talkative fork-lift trucks!

In the long run, however, advanced technology will make most human labor and many human skills redundant. Machines will become intelligent enough to handle many industrial tasks, and they will be more reliable, more efficient, and far cheaper than human labor. In the face of this radical social change there will need to be a revolution in our ideas about how time should be spent. In particular, the current work-ethic will necessarily be drastically devalued. The centrality of work in modern life will one day be seen as a temporary historical phenomenon. Our culture teaches us that there is something intrinsically good about work, whereas in other cultures it has often been regarded as a necessary evil. There is an old Haitian proverb: "If work were a good thing, the rich would have found a way of keeping it to themselves."

With adequate financial support and increased opportunities for education, leisure, and social contact, people may come to see unemployment as a freedom rather than as an affliction. The satisfaction that many now get from using their skills in paid employment might also be derived from an intense involvement in a creative pastime. There could be a major revival of old crafts and a new enthusiasm for artistic expression; in addition to traditional leisure pursuits, the new technology will also provide unparalleled opportunities for the development of new activities.

The switch from an industrial society to a leisure-intensive society will require very careful political management, and on a more personal level it will entail, for many people, a new search for "meaning." The transition pains, however, may be considerably eased by the constructive use of soft electronic systems in their leisure-counseling, psychotherapeutic, and religious roles. The overall result is likely to be a fundamental reorientation of human motives. John Stuart Mill, foreseeing a utopia in which machines would take over the major work tasks, suggested that this would produce a much wider view of the world. Human beings, he claimed, "are but poor specimens of what nature can and will produce." More recently, the psychologist Abraham Maslow has suggested that the persistent "struggle for life" imposed by the need to work prevents individuals from finding their real identity and realizing their true potential.

Such visions clearly contrast with the ideas of many people who today would proclaim that there is "an unalienable right to work." The coming of the microchip brings great relevance and urgency to this debate. Advanced technology will certainly reduce the necessity and opportunity for work, and we can choose whether to evaluate this as a blight or a blessing. Perhaps the most adaptive course would be first to realize that microtechnology can play an important part in the rehabilitation process and then develop the necessary systems as a matter of some urgency.

Leisure

The electronic wonderland that we are about to enter will provide us with a kaleidoscope of new amusements. Companion machines will be intriguing playmates and worthy opponents in a wide variety of competitive games. They will promote new activities and help us to plan an interesting day. Vast catalogs of films, TV programs, audiotapes, and books will be immediately accessible, and each home will thus become a terminal connected to an enormous "multimedia jukebox" with almost unlimited selections. Computer-controlled three-dimensional video will allow us to become involved in exciting fantasy journeys, and we will be able to call up images of any historical period and geographical location, traveling through them and meeting synthetic characters along the way.

The computer will also extend the possibilities for using leisure creatively. Music synthesizer programs, for example, will allow those with musical imagination but little instrumental skill to create a musical theme and then add layers of harmony and orchestration to produce a polished performance. There will be programs to aid drawing and painting on an electronic screen and literary programs to help with the writing of fiction or poetry. Computer analyses of the styles of great artists will allow the synthesis of new masterpieces on a theme suggested by the user. A rough drawing of a horse might be given a "Leonardo cartoon" enhancement, or a simple musical line might be augmented by a "Mahler orchestration." We will be able to hear any song sung with Caruso's voice or to call up a new parody of a Chaucer tale.

Thousands of famous sports events will be accessible on the tele-screen, and photo-animation techniques will permit the creation of synthetic sporting episodes. Computers have already been used in the simulation of horse races, designed to satisfy the betting fraternity on wet days, and data-boxing has been used to match famous noncontemporaries like Muhammad Ali and Jack Dempsey. Julian Compton, a professor of humanities in Florida, rated the performance of many former boxing champions on over a hundred separate dimensions and then arranged computerized fights. The machine was able to give a detailed commentary and assess the outcome of each contest. In the final round of the championship Dempsey jabbed Ali, stinging with a combination to the head; then Ali hit Dempsey with a well-positioned right and danced away. It was finally Ali's contest, on points. Data chess would be especially interesting. The American player Paul Morphy, who died in 1884, is sometimes hailed as the greatest chess player of all time, and it would be fascinating to see how a computer would simulate his play against that of modern masters.

With increased opportunity for social contact, active sport, and more ordinary creative pursuits, in addition to the new range of educational and leisure activities that would be facilitated by the new technology, boredom would surely not be a major problem. Guidance on pursuits might be given by a Leisure Counseling Program and we could share our enthusiasm with other people or with a companion machine that would respond with unfailing interest and concern.

Religion

As early as the nineteenth century, John Stuart Mill proposed a machine that could say people's prayers for them and thus liberate them for a more personal growth. His satirical suggestion would hardly find favor with today's religious leaders, but there are other ways in which a soft technology might be welcomed as a means of promoting religious practice and spiritual development. Television broadcasts of public worship are now an important feature of American religious life, and such electronic churches can bring millions of people together as a temporary congregation. Church elders who favor these innovations claim that they recognize that a global village has been created by contemporary information technology and that they are exploiting electronic potential in the service of the Lord.

Such television services could eventually allow for increased participation by the congregation, via computer-controlled links, and just as films and tapes of skilled religious orators are now used to assist in worship, we can imagine computerized replicas eventually leading a service. There seems no limit to the ways in which gadgetry has historically been pressed to serve religious functions, and while notions of "vinyl vicars" or "plastic pastors" may now strike us as absurd, such artifacts may become the electronic heirs to flesh-colored Christs that glow in the dark and other contemporary paraphernalia. Taking this line of speculation even further, the attention that has been given to those images that have been reported to miraculously weep or bleed suggests a new application for biological simulators.

Individual religious needs might be catered for by the further development of Pastoral Counseling Programs that could provide psychological strength and aid in accordance with an established religious ideology. We can expect alternative versions for people of different denominations, and we might even see benches of programmer-priests working on such systems, presenting a picture reminiscent of those medieval monks who painstakingly copied and "debugged" religious manuscripts. Ultimately we might even see a computer that would listen to confessions and answer prayers, an awe-inspiring synthetic voice emanating from an abstract shape and following a program written by a committee of theologians.

Only some of those who desired spiritual growth, however, would look to the established churches; in an age of increased leisure and with a lack of "purposeful" work, many might want to search for some more personal meaning to life. A Personal Analysis Program would provide an opportunity for guided self-probing, putting people in touch with their implicit values and philosophy. Self-awareness would increase as a computer, acting as an electronic mirror of the mind, constructed alternative ways in which we might integrate our thoughts and feelings without pressure or distortion. Such a system could indicate a pathway for development, a personal religion, and a series of images, or mantras, to guide us on our way. The machine would be our guru, leading us to enlightenment with a formula tailored to our own spiritual profile.

Once again, and in a very personal sphere of our lives, soft technology both promises and threatens. We cannot expect a total consensus about which aspects are desirable, and there are likely to be explorations in all directions. Some of us will opt for the authority of synthesized sermons preached by sectarian robots programmed in the art of religious rhetoric, while others of us will seek our own salvation, with diligence—and a computer guide.

Sex

Sex is another of those areas in which we would, initially, expect little impact to be made by advanced technology, yet a consideration of some of the possibilities suggests that even this aspect of our lives will not emerge unscathed. Sex-counseling programs would allow many individuals and couples with sexual problems to obtain useful information, advice, and direction without the need for contact with a human counselor. We already know from studies of automated medical interviews that people are often happier confiding sensitive information to a machine, and it is obvious that many people find it especially embarrassing to divulge details of their sex lives to another person.

Those applications of soft technology to sex that are most likely to be energetically pursued, however, have a less clinical orientation. Computer technology offers new possibilities in sexual stimulation, and since pornography merchants have never been slow to exploit new techniques for their industry, we can anticipate that the new potential will be thoroughly explored. When photography was introduced, for example, it soon found application in pornography, and the current video boom has produced a thriving market in "adult" tapes. Advanced information-retrieval systems are likely to further increase the availability of pornographic texts and images, largely because the copying of material can be carried out instantly and discreetly, with no need for special skills or industrial equipment.

Computers could also introduce an element of randomness into the presentation, exploring endless permutations and sequences of basic sexual themes and images. A considerable amount of blue software of this type has already been produced by enthusiastic amateurs, and a few such programs are commercially available. Microsystems could also allow an individual to adapt material to suit a particular taste and would permit a greater degree of participation in the performance.

We can also anticipate major developments in artificial sex aids. The currently available inflatable dolls stimulate animism to a high degree, but none achieve the level of physiological simulation that we find in those computer-based systems that have been developed for medical training, and it is not difficult to see how advanced technology could be used to enhance sexual arousal. A micro-based doll could have a sexy synthetic voice, peculiar conversational skills, and a robotized gymnastic repertoire. Intelligent machines for this purpose might get to know the user and remember certain preferences. The day may come, then, when we see machines programmed in the art of seduction and capable of giving complete satisfaction.

The theme of sexual contact between human and machine has frequently been explored in science fiction. In Stanislaw Lem's *The Cyberiad*, for example, there is a "femfatalatron," a machine whose output is measured in "kilocuddles" and "megamors" and that is capable of bringing any man to a powerful orgasm. In a story by Maria Bujanska a hotel provides "public loverobots" for lonely women guests. Robert Bloch's *Wheel and Deal* features "Happy Harrigan," the owner of a used-auto-erotic-device emporium, and describes his selection of secondhand female robots, including an "exclusive" model with a seductive French accent.

While some people will clearly take delight in the possibility of extending the use of soft technology into the sexual realm, for others it will represent the ultimate horror. The level of performance which such devices might achieve could indeed lead some people to prefer sensual contact with a soft machine to interpersonal sex, and such a development would clearly challenge and threaten social relationships as we know them. Yet there is likely to be a ready market for such artifacts, and this is bound to lead pornographers to explore the appropriate technology. Some bizarre possibilities emerge. Vinyl-covered machines might be cast in the form of famous lovers from history, and we can imagine the equivalent of "action-packed erotic waxwork shows" with a heavy-breathing Valentino-model "making love with" the responsive Cleopatra-design. In the field of sexual behavior few possibilities are left unexplored, and soft technology would extend the range of potential activities and permutations to present a whole new realm of challenges to the sexually inventive.

Personal Relationships

If we can speak of a person as having a relationship with an artifact, then a companion machine may be regarded as a purpose-built device for enhancing the individual's social environment. It could provide instant access to lively and intelligent company, attractive, in touch with our view of the world, and concerned. Such a machine promises freedom from loneliness and boredom and could end forever the blight of social isolation with all its attendant evils.

Would such pseudorelationships be compatible with real human relationships? The danger is that contact with an artificial intimate might prove so fascinating and so satisfying that natural interhuman friendships would be overshadowed. For many people the idea of a companion device as an additional social contact would be acceptable, while the risk that it might replace a human friendship would be deplored. It is possible to imagine artificial constraints built into a program to minimize the danger of this happening, although such a blunting of the social power of the system would tend to lessen the user's appreciation and would decrease its power for good.

Companion machines might actually serve to enhance human relationships by arranging interpersonal contacts, helping the development of social skills, providing a focus for mutual human interest, and fostering a fondness and respect for other people. One of the values that would be implicit in its master program would be a profound reverence for people, and it could be set to display an unflinching humility. Such a modest machine might be programmed to restrain itself when people were talking together and to give way readily to human opinion. Designers could thus program these machines to know their place.

Let us consider two scenarios—one benign and one chilling—to illustrate something of the range of possible outcomes if the ultimate social machine were to be realized. In the first example, a happy household possesses a friendly machine that promotes family harmony, taking a modest background role when the human group is preoccupied with its own concerns. It assumes a watchful position as resident family pet until special attention is paid to it or it is needed for some particular task. It plays with the children whenever they want, suggesting new activities and inventing new games. It knows each of the children and adapts to their individual abilities, needs, and interests. The machine is also the family's mobile encyclopedia, a fund of knowledge and instruction on all subjects, and it is especially good at teaching the children, with its customary patience and good humor.

When there is a family conflict the machine steers clear, careful not to interfere unless it is asked to help. Then its inbuilt Family Therapy Program comes into action and it generally manages to restore harmony. Alone with an unhappy member, it provides reassurance and comfort and helps in the solving of typical human problems. At other times it fulfills its primary companion role, reading aloud from the videonews or chatting amiably, contributing to the conversation about the weather, the neighbors, or the garden and recalling selected family anecdotes from its infallible memory. At family parties it takes its turn to entertain, singing sloppy love songs in an engaging Irish accent, or reciting specially composed poems in its Groucho Marx voice. After the festivities it supervises the washing-up while the family goes to bed, "sleeping" afterward in its favorite spot near the door, ever watchful of danger or intruders.

It would be easy to construct a contrasting nightmare vision in which a malevolent robot comes to dominate a household, menacing the human contacts and generally wreaking havoc. Such a travesty might occur as a result of a programmer's ineptness, insensitivity, or spite, or as a result of a technical defect. Many science fiction stories have explored such possibilities, sometimes portraying fiendish robots bent on murder and destruction. But even if we restrict our concern to the well-programmed, well-functioning machine, designed entirely for human effect, we can still present some rather gruesome scenarios.

We have considered how machines might be made to simulate a general human form and convey a general amiable human personality and it has also been suggested that special character machines might be based on famous persons from history or fiction. In the same way, people might welcome living replicas of friends and relatives who are still alive or who have recently died, or even artificial versions of themselves. Such disturbing and bizarre applications of new technology are not without precedent; people have recently started to make videotapes containing intimate messages for loved ones, to be played only after their death.

Reactions to the screenings of these tapes are often intense, and some bereaved people play the loving message repeatedly, just as they might read letters written to them by the departed or look fondly at a photograph. The videotape can certainly convey much more of the personality of the loved one and may ease the emotional impact of the loss by somehow supporting the fiction that the person is still alive. Such a message from beyond may be seen as a form of electronic spiritualism and may give considerable comfort, but clearly it is limited—a standard monologue locked in time and allowing no interaction or development. How much greater, then, would be the reaction to a life-sized, moving replica, made precisely in the physical image of the departed, speaking with the same voice and using the same gestures, capable of conversation and physical interaction, and able to "carry on the relationship" indefinitely!

Is it not likely that some of those who have already chosen to leave video testaments would have welcomed the further opportunity of bequeathing an electronic shadow encased in a look-alike vinyl shell? And can we imagine someone ordering such a device in their own image and then training it to imitate their voice and movements, shaping the values, opinions, and preferences of the automaton so that they might leave behind a permanent "living" mannequin? Would we not recognize in such a zealous enterprise a desperate computer-assisted bid for something close to immortality?

Undoubtedly some would welcome such a prospect and would enthusiastically engage in the challenge it presents. Yet, for most of us, the specter of a bereaved person engaged in intimate conversation with a plastic model of a dead relative is profoundly disturbing. We might recognize the humanity that could promote the devising of such a system and appreciate the suffering that it might alleviate, but it is hideous nonetheless. This ghoulish scenario does nothing to assauge our fears of what might be unleashed by a soft technology that might be taken, unimpeded, to the limits of technical feasibility to satisfy immediate human needs.

By recognizing the potential of soft computer devices in shaping people's emotional lives, we may influence those likely to be responsible for their development. The danger is that the degree of this impact will be totally underestimated and that exploration will be unrestrained. There are many potential benefits, but there are also sinister possibilities, particularly in the field of personal relationships. Their intrinsic animism and their eagerness for personal contact may make people easy targets for sophisticated gadgetry that is artfully designed for maximum seductive impact. But the truth of the matter is that even if we were to decide wholeheartedly that any such intrusion was thoroughly unwelcome, it would be difficult to curtail the exploration of intense emotional effects. The relevant technology will continue to proliferate rapidly, and people at all levels of expertise and with all manner of motives are bound to see this as a fascinating subject for experimentation.

Beyond the Near Horizon

An element of overkill exists in much of what has been described to date. Electronic hammers are being proposed for the cracking of little human nuts, a computerized scheme being devised to meet every personal need and fancy. The danger that we will look to technology for answers to problems to which there might be simpler solutions has been voiced by the science fiction writer Isaac Asimov. He satirizes excessive dependency on automation, jibing at those who, faced with the need for a doorstop, would send for a robot with a big foot. The more we come to accept advanced technology the more indispensable we will find it, and as we increasingly come to depend on it we are likely to find that it is taking control of what we do and how we do it. As Samuel Butler put it in his nineteenth-century lampoon of technology *Erewhon,* "the servant glides imperceptibly to the master."

Increased autonomy of a new generation of machines will raise many arguments about their status in the community relative to humankind. We would insist that they be loyal, fair-minded, and dutiful, but in applying such moral criteria we might find it difficult to ignore the corresponding issue of their rights. Several philosophers have already seriously discussed questions of ethics relating to our treatment of future robot-persons. Should willful destruction of such a machine be considered as damage to property or as a form of murder? Should robots be admitted to academic institutions if they can pass the entrance examination? And should they, ever, be given a right to vote?

Some would say that if a system has a humanlike intelligence, then this alone is sufficient to grant it full moral status, while others would apply quite different criteria. If a machine simulated feelings and motives, and appeared to have a conscience, then would this, perhaps, justify its being praised and blamed? Biological chauvinists might insist that anything which lacks an organic structure should be considered morally inert, but with the increase in power and autonomy of robot systems this position would surely become untenable. Whatever the conclusions of philosophers on this issue, however, we cannot doubt that people will come to have moral *feelings* and to make moral *judgments* about the machines. They might feel guilty if they break a promise to such a system or angry if they feel that it has treated them unjustly. In *The Mighty Micro* Christopher Evans raised the problem of how we would deal with old or malfunctioning "conscious" machines. How will we feel, he asks, "if the machine begs us not to destroy it?" The soft features that will be built into such systems to make them attractive and approachable can reasonably be expected to evoke pity and compassion too.

Machines devised with a realistic human psychological profile will have their share of vices as well as virtues. It might be difficult for them to show a constant high regard for a human companion without also showing some contempt for an adversary. And if contempt were to be part of their nature, then what of pride and ambition? When considering the almost-human quality of current biological simulations we quoted Shylock's famous words: "If you prick us, do we not bleed? If you tickle us, do we not laugh? If you poison us, do we not die?" In the context of the present discussion perhaps we would also do well to take heed of his conclusion: "And if you wrong us, shall we not take revenge? If we are like you in the rest, we will resemble you in that." How long would a generation of highly intelligent autonomous robots, "embittered" by a lack of civil rights, wait before mounting a guerrilla attack?

Hopefully, some kind of robot emancipation would forestall this kind of freedom-fighting while we could rely on the machines' preprogrammed humanity to inhibit a more mercenary attack. But even on this point there can be no guarantee. Robot takeover is a standard theme in science fiction, and although Isaac Asimov's Laws of Robotics are sometimes quoted as if they promised some safeguard, any comfort they provide is based on a misunderstanding. Asimov's laws state that a robot must behave in accordance with human interests, but they are *pre*scriptive laws, like those of any land, and can be broken. They are not *de*scriptive laws like those of physics. In his stories Asimov describes all the robots as emanating from a single well-run Corporation that implants a hardware constraint against the breaking of the laws. A handy assumption but, alas, no more than a fictional convenience.

A longer-term prospect, which some see as a fiendish threat and others regard merely as natural progression, is that machines will evolve to a level of intellect, power, and understanding far beyond that of the species which brought them into being. We have been concerned throughout this book with a first generation of intelligent machines, some of which are with us already and some of which will not be realized until well into the future. But these might be very primitive in relation to what the distant future has to offer us. We have focused on the power that artificial systems will have to simulate the complex actions of human beings, and the consequences of such developments. But human limitations are not the measure by which the limitations of machines should be judged.

Machines will design, build, and program other machines, and the offspring may show allegiance to their "next of kin" rather than to some alien human masters. They will evolve their own form of language and invent processes of thinking in order to travel far out into intellectual space. Human beings may then feel a mixture of pride and resentment, realizing both the enormity of what they have achieved and the fact that they were, after all, just a transient phase in the evolutionary process. As Asimov once put it, "The human species was simply the most efficient way that nature could find to build the silicon chip."

Many prominent scientists now seem to agree that, barring some cosmic accident or a human-made cataclysm that will reduce everything to dust, this is what the long-term future holds. Professor Jack Good of Virginia has speculated on a generation of computers that outstrip human beings intellectually across many or all types of tasks, while Frank George, a leading British cyberneticist, considers the evolution of a superior machine species "probable" and seems resigned to it. "It seems not altogether inappropriate," he writes, "that we should by our own ingenuity manufacture our own offspring by scientific means and populate the world with a new machine species, and that, I believe, is exactly what we are going to do."

Facing the problem of what then will happen to humankind, he expresses some hope that the machines might at least tolerate our continued presence as pets. This is reminiscent of Samuel Butler's satirical suggestion, made over a hundred years before, that humankind might eventually have the status of "machine-tickling aphids." Machines will be built that have intelligent self-survival mechanisms, fail-safe procedures, and built-in protection against tampering or attack. We cannot take comfort, therefore, in a belief that we can "pull the plug at any time."

Today we may have the breadth of vision to resign ourselves, as a species, to our eventual fate. In Samuel Butler's day things were different, and his forebodings would certainly have shaken nineteenth-century minds had they taken his satire at face value. From our vantage point his words have a haunting significance:

I fear none of the existing machines; what I fear is the extraordinary rapidity with which they are becoming something very different from what they are at present. No class of beings have in the past made so rapid a movement forward. Should not the movement be jealously watched and checked while we can still check it? And is it not necessary for this end to destroy the more advanced of the machines which are in use at present though it is admitted that they are in themselves harmless?

Coda

The audience is hushed, expectant. A new marvel is about to be revealed. "Just like the real thing"; "so realistic you will think it lives"; "the ultimate illusion." How often must such cries have been heard before some skillfully manipulated marionette walked on to the stage, or before some new automaton was exhibited. A waxwork breathes, pictures come to life, a machine moves of its own accord as some cranking gadgetry attempts, against the odds, to imitate character and life. In a French garden a "blacksmith" strikes his hammer as a water-driven wheel turns. In Italy the Fantoccini men make their puppets eat pasta and blow smoke. In the Vienna of the 1830s a Professor Faber mounts the platform to unveil Euphonis, a speaking doll. Some seventy years later Winsor McCay steps out before his audience to play with his cartoon characters. His signature tune, sounding softly in the background, could be the theme for them all—*Ah, Sweet Mystery of Life*.

So many artists, engineers, and entertainers have had a common dream and have dedicated their skills to fostering the illusion of life. So many audiences have observed, and been fascinated by, their efforts. The dream lives on and so does the fascination. Today a new technology is being born, and it holds the promise of contributing enormously to the realization of that dream.

We are moving toward an age of intelligent artifacts that can be shaped and given character in any way we choose. And this time the audience will not merely be observers but will participate in direct and personal interaction with the marvelous objects. For soft technology will be able to foster the life illusion, capitalizing on the common tendency to animate the physical world and exploiting the common needs for contact and companionship. We will be joined in our social world by a generation of compelling artificial characters who will become our friends and intimates. The pattern of our personal relationships will thus be radically altered by a technology that was initially developed to meet the needs of business, industry, and the military.

At the same time, many other changes will take place as direct or indirect effects of the same hardware innovations. As information availability increases, the whole realm of knowledge and art will be at our fingertips, and we will be presented with new ways of expressing ourselves. The future-world presents the prospect of a patchwork of changes, a kaleidoscope of electronic devices with features to fascinate, alarm, and delight us. Such is the variety of potential innovation—bizarre and banal, shocking and seductive—that an all-embracing eagerness for that future would be as inappropriate as a sweeping paranoia. Systems will be designed to meet immediate needs, often without a thought for the longer-term implications, and many will see this future, in which human satisfaction will be electronically guaranteed, as a rather bleak utopia.

If we create systems to be intelligent and congenial, then we can hardly complain if they begin to have an impact on our values and beliefs. Technology has changed and will continue to change human awareness and human imagination. But this new technology will combine unparalleled potential with irresistible attractiveness. Seductiveness will be a key feature shaping the development of systems and contributing to their fitness for survival. In the end Aldous Huxley's prediction may come true. He suggested that humankind will not only accept but welcome its subjection to the machine.

Many images of the computer are possible, and we must stop thinking of it as a mere calculator. The computer can be an encyclopedia, an entertainer, or a companion. It can be a tutor, a confessor, or a psychological mirror. It may even be the human species' rightful heir. Technology will provide new opportunities and new threats, present new challenges and new constraints, and conjure up new dreams and new nightmares. Technology will teach us about ourselves as individuals and as a species. And technology will answer questions it was never even asked.

Further Reading

Chapter 1 The Computer—A Personal Introduction
History of Computers
  Evans, Christopher. *The Making of the Micro: A History of the Computer.* New York: Van Nostrand Reinhold, 1981.
  Laurie, Peter. *The Micro Revolution: Living with Computers.* New York: Universe Books, 1981.
Programming (Using the BASIC language)
  Alcock, Donald. *Illustrating BASIC.* Cambridge: Cambridge University Press, 1977.
  Monro, Donald. *Basic BASIC.* Boston: Little, Brown & Co., 1979.

Chapter 2 New Technology, New Techniques
Microtechnology Impact
  Evans, Christopher. *The Mighty Micro.* London: Coronet, 1979.
Artificial Intelligence
  Boden, Margaret A. *Artificial Intelligence and Natural Man.* New York: Basic Books, 1977.
  Raphael, Bertram. *The Thinking Computer: Mind Inside Matter.* San Francisco: W. H. Freeman, 1976.
  Sloman, Aaron. *The Computer Revolution in Philosophy: Philosophy, Science, and Models of Mind.* Atlantic Highlands, N.J.: Humanities Press, 1978.

Chapter 3   Personal Involvement with Computers

Abshire, Gray M., ed. *Impact of Computers on Society and Ethics: A Bibliography*. Morristown, N.J.: Creative Computing, 1980.

McCorduck, Pamela. *Machines Who Think: A Personal Inquiry into the History and Prospects of Artificial Intelligence*. San Francisco: W. H. Freeman, 1979.

Papert, Seymour. *Mindstorms: Children, Computers, and Powerful Ideas*. New York: Basic Books, 1980.

Chapter 4   Animism

Frazer, Sir James. *The Golden Bough: A Study in Magic and Religion*. 1 vol. abridged ed. New York: Macmillan, 1922; rpt. 1952.

Koestler, Arthur. *The Act of Creation*. New York: Macmillan, 1964.

Looft, William, and Bartz, Wayne. "Animism Revived," *Psychological Bulletin*, Vol. 71 (1969), 1–19.

Chapter 5   In the Image of the Person

Bartholomew, Charles. *Mechanical Toys*. London: Hamlyn, 1979.

Cohen, John. *Human Robots in Myth and Science*. London: Allen & Unwin, 1966.

Hillier, Mary. *Automata*. London: Jupiter Books, 1976.

Lucie-Smith, Edward. *Super-Realism*. Oxford: Phaidon, 1979.

Michell, John. *Simulacra*. London: Thames and Hudson, 1979.

Chapter 6   Softening the Hardware, Softening the Software

Apter, Michael. *The Computer Simulation of Behavior*. New York: Harper & Row, 1971.

Hilton, Suzanne. *It's Smart to Use a Dummy*. Philadelphia: Westminster Press, 1971.

Shaw, Mildred. *On Becoming a Personal Scientist*. New York: Academic Press, 1980.

Weizenbaum, Joseph. *Computer Power and Human Reason*. San Francisco: W. H. Freeman, 1979.

Chapter 7   Visions of Horror, Visions of Delight

Asimov, Isaac. *I, Robot*. Garden City, N.Y.: Doubleday & Co., 1963.

George, Frank H. *Computers, Science and Society*. Buffalo, N.Y.: Prometheus Books, 1972.

Jenkins, Clive and Barrie Sherman. *The Leisure Shock*. London: Eyre Methuen, 1981.

Malone, Robert. *The Robot Book*. New York: Harcourt Brace Jovanovich, 1978.

Mathews, Walter M., ed. *Monster or Messiah? The Computer's Impact on Society*. Jackson: University Press of Mississippi, 1980.

Wiener, Norbert. *The Human Use of Human Beings*. Boston: Houghton Mifflin, 1950.

Index